YOUR FUTURE

**An A-Z index
to prophecy**

by Dr. Jack Van Impe

Printed in the United States of America.

Third Printing 1994

Jack Van Impe Ministries
P.O. Box 7004 • Troy, Michigan 48007
In Canada: Box 1717, Postal Station A
Windsor, Ontario, N9A 6Y1

ISBN 0-934803-68-4

FOREWORD

Prophecy is history written in advance. The omniscient, all-knowing God knows the future as well as the past and present. Acts 15:18 declares, *Known unto God are all his works from the beginning of the world.* God cannot err in the minutest detail. That makes prophecy reliable because it is not simply the predictions of prophets that are recorded in the Bible, but the very words of God to men. Peter, in his second book, chapter 1, verse 21, emphasizes this fact by saying, *For the prophecy came not in old time by the will of man: but holy men of God spake as they were moved by the Holy Ghost.*

My interest in this subject began when our family was converted through a booklet emphasizing Christ's return at the time of World War II. Later, I became acquainted with the late Dr. L. Sale Harrison, a prophetical giant, as we ministered together at Bible conferences. Over the years, great prophetic scholars such as Dr. M. R. DeHaan, Dr. John Walvoord, and Dr. Dwight Pentecost were instrumental in enlightening me further as to the great truths of the prophetic Word.

For 54 years I have preached prophecy 25 percent of the time. One in every four messages has been on this glorious theme. This is normal as one in every four verses within God's Word deals with eschatology. In fact, there are 20 verses about the return of Christ for every verse concerning Christ's incarnation (His coming as a babe into Bethlehem's manger).

I am grateful to Margaret Reese, wife of Dr. Ed Reese, the editor of the *Chronological Bible*, for searching, researching, and placing materials from scores of my books into computers to find and arrange the alphabetical listing contained herein. This was an extensive project because of its enormity and forms the foundation and superstructure for this volume.

I am also exceptionally appreciative for the additional insight received from the writings of Dr. J. Dwight Pentecost and Rev. Donald R. Rouse. Our ministry has promoted Dr. Pentecost's book, *Things to Come*, for a number of years. It is a comprehensive, all inclusive study on prophecy. Dr. John F. Walvoord commenting on this book in its introduction states: "Though many learned men have written in the field of eschatology to provide that which is usually lacking in standard theologies, few, if any, have attempted a detailed presentation of premillennial eschatology such as is provided in this volume. Dr. Pentecost has, with rare skill, dealt with many controversial issues, has met and solved many prophetic problems, and has provided in large measure the substance of the prophetic Word in systematic and theological form. He has condensed a mass of material often not contained in even larger prophetic libraries. The work as a whole merits classification as a standard and comprehensive text on Biblical Eschatology."

Rev. Donald R. Rouse has published *The Bible Student's Dictionary of Prophetic Terms* and has done a superb job in categorizing, classifying, and clarifying prophetical terminology.

May the blessed Holy Spirit who illuminated my mind, also open your spiritual eyes to the great prophetical truths contained in this book.

ABADDON

This is the name of a chief angel of Satan whose domain is the bottomless pit. In Hebrew, *Abaddon* signifies "the place of destruction personified." In the Greek, *Abaddon* is called "Apollyon."

Abaddon is used also as a parallel with Sheol (Job 26:6, Proverbs 15:11; 27:20), with death (Job 28:22), and with the grave (Psalm 88:11).

ABOMINATION OF DESOLATION

The Antichrist will take control of Jewish worship midway through the Tribulation, declaring himself to be God (2 Thessalonians 2:4) and demanding worship from the Jews in their own Temple, even to the point of setting up an Image of the Beast therein. This image of the unholy one is the abomination that renders desolate all Jewish hopes (Daniel 12:11; Matthew 24:15-22). The true Jewish heart will be broken, because idolatry is forbidden in the Ten Commandments (Exodus 20:4). This act precipitates the judgment of God as the Temple fills with smoke and seven angels come out carrying seven plagues. The voice of Almighty God issues forth from the smoke-filled Temple, directing the angels to carry out their duties. His holiness has been offended. Mankind has worshipped a man, Antichrist, the devil in human skin . . . even bowing to his image (Matthew 24:15; Isaiah 42:8; Exodus 20:4-6). Mankind, en masse, has grossly violated God's commandment about images during the Tribulation period and promised judgment must begin (Isaiah 42:8; Exodus 20:4-6).

(See also Image of the Beast)

ABRAHAM, SEED OF (See Seed of Abraham)

ABRAHAMIC COVENANT (See Covenants)

ABRAHAM'S BOSOM

A place of comfort to which the angels carried Lazarus upon his death (Luke 16:22). It is equivalent to Paradise (see Hades). All God's people went there until Calvary.

Abraham's Bosom, the comfort side of Hades, was evacuated after Christ's crucifixion and resurrection when Christ descended into the lower parts of the earth and ascended, taking His people waiting there to the third heaven (where all saints presently go at death) (Ephesians 4:8-10; 2 Corinthians 12:2-5).

ABYSS (See Bottomless Pit)

AEON

Aeon (age), frequently translated "world," evil in its tendency, is essentially a time word. It is often used in the sense of eternity, the sum total of all the ages (Matthew 6:13; Luke 1:33,55; John 6:51,58; 8:35; 12:34; Romans 9:5; 11:36; 2 Corinthians 9:9; Philippians 4:20; Hebrews 7:17,21; 1 Peter 1:25; Revelation 15:7).

AGE

A period of time of indefinite duration (Acts 15:18) recognized by its characteristics and events (Mark 4:19; 1 Corinthians 2:6; Galatians 1:4; Ephesians 2:2; 2 Timothy 4:10).

Note the differences between:

"Before the ages": before time began, or eternity past (1 Corinthians 2:7).

"Ages past": that span of time which ended with Christ's coming (Colossians 1:26; Ephesians 3:5).

"This present age": the time in which we are now living, ending with the Second Coming of Christ (Matthew 12:32; 13:39,40,49; Ephesians 1:21). This age witnesses the inception, development, and completion of God's purpose in *taking out . . . a people for his name* (Acts 15:14).

"Ages to come": endless time, eternity future (Ephesians 2:7).

AGE OF GRACE (See Church Age)

AGES, PROGRAM OF THE

God has divided His program into time segments to evidence the progress of divine revelation through successive ages. There are many passages indicating God has a program for the ages (Deuteronomy 30:1-10; Daniel 2:31-45; 7:1-28; 9:24-27; Hosea 3:4,5; Matthew 23:37-25:46; Acts 15:13-18; Romans 11:13-29; 2 Thessalonians 3:1-12; Revelations 2:1-22:31).

Christ is the very center of that program (Hebrews 1:1,2; 9:26; Timothy 1:17; 1 Corinthians 10:11). Therefore, the ages are the time periods within which God is revealing His divine purpose and program as it centers in the Lord Jesus Christ.

AIR POWER (See Signs)

ALLEGORY (See Interpretation, Methods)

AMERICA

There are a number of chapters within God's Word that seem to picture the USA. No other nation throughout history can so convincingly fulfill all of the requirements of the texts. America is certainly included in the judgments upon all nations (Ezekiel 39:21). America also seems to be the political Babylon of Revelation 18. God's Word mentions three Babylons: a city (Genesis 11), a church (Revelation 17), and a country (Revelation 18). Don't confuse the three (see Babylon).

Isaiah, Jeremiah, and John describe this country:

Isaiah 18:1,2 — America's emblem, with outstretched wings; beyond the sea from Israel; a nation, scattered and peeled, meaning spread out and cultured; measured or staked out and polluted in its waterways.

Jeremiah 50 — Here she is called the heritage of the Lord and faces judgment because of her backsliding (vs. 11). A nation of mingled people (vs. 37); a nation whose coexisting "mother" (England) is confounded at the hour of her decline (vs. 12).

Jeremiah 51 — In this text America is bordered by the

9

world's two largest oceans and possesses its longest river (vs. 13); her wealth plagues the nations to jealousy (vs. 7); her space exploits are fantastic (vs. 53).

John pictures two Babylons in Revelation. One is a world religion (chapter 17), the other an internationally respected nation (vs. 3); laden with sin (vs. 5), with a superabundance of material goods producing idleness and sin (vs. 7).

America today is surely laden with iniquity with its drunkenness, drug addiction, tobacco, gambling, prostitution, homosexuality, smut peddlers, immorality, abortions, mercy killers, murderers, robbers, and looters. There is specific judgment administered against Babylon, identified as America. A sneak attack is predicted in Jeremiah 50:24 and in one hour Babylon is destroyed (Revelation 18:10). Some biblical scholars believe that Russia starts the sneak nuclear attack against the USA, crippling her, and then against Israel (Ezekiel 39:2). Whatever the alignment of events, it is clear that both nations fall, Christ returns, and world peace begins (see Babylon).

AMILLENNIALISM
This teaching states that there is no Millennium, denying Isaiah 11:7 and scores of other Old Testament texts. Those who believe this allegorize, symbolize, or figuratize scriptural texts.

ANGELS
Sometimes referred to as stars, these beings are God's messengers in the prophetic timetable. They announce events, pronounce judgments, and carry out God's wishes (they represent the seven churches in Revelation 1 and 2 and are often found praising the Lamb for His many attributes (Revelation 5). Angels take the lead in the praise and worship of God and rejoice with each crisis in the onward march of events to the consumma-

tion of the kingdom. Although they have never known conflict, sin, pardon, and victory, they rejoice over those who have and give glory to God for His grace. After the Resurrection at the last trump, they seem to fade from the scene as the heavenly redeemed sit down on thrones and exercise judgment with the Lord Jesus at His coming (1 Corinthians 6:2,3; Matthew 12:28).

Appearances of Christ (Theophanies and Christophanies) are found throughout the Old Testament, usually in the form of angelic manifestations (Isaiah 63:9). Christ appears again in angelic form in Revelation 7:2,3; 8:5; and 10:1.

ANGELS, FALLEN

Apparently, fallen angels (angelic followers of Satan) also known as demons, will be very active during the Tribulation (Revelation 12). They are also referred to as stars (Revelation 12:4). Satan, himself, is also an angelic being and appears as one in Revelation 9:1,11, opening the bottomless pit and releasing his demons (the convicts of the ages) in the form of hideous creatures to torture mankind. They will be judged by Christ after the Tribulation, before the Millennium (1 Corinthians 6:3).

ANGELS, JUDGMENT OF (See Judgment of Angels)

ANIMAL SACRIFICES (See Millennial Sacrifices)

ANTICHRIST, THE

Before Christ returns to set up His kingdom of peace, Satan will enter a man's body and present his counterfeit, the Antichrist, as the Messiah. This internationally deified dictator will inaugurate a world peace program which holds the world spellbound for 42 months, or three and one-half years. When the world believes utopia has arrived, the bottom falls out. In the middle of the seven-year period of Tribulation, the Antichrist breaks all of his pledges and destroys his contractual obligations with Israel (Daniel 9:27; 1 Thessalonians 5:3). He will come out of an amalgamation of ten Western nations (Daniel 9:26). He will meet his Waterloo when he is cast into the Lake of Fire with the False Prophet after Jesus Christ conquers him at Armageddon (Revelation 19:20).

Other names attributed to Antichrist:

Little horn (Daniel 7:8). The "little horn" arises out of the fourth beast which represents Rome. It is likely that Antichrist will rise out of the revived Roman Empire. This term is also used of Antiochus Epiphanes in Daniel 8:9.

King of fierce countenance (Daniel 8:23). Antichrist will be a cruel ruler, trampling men under foot without fear of God. He is also called *the willful king* (Daniel 11:36).

The prince that shall come (Daniel 9:26). The people of the coming prince are the ones who will *destroy the city and the sanctuary*. The Romans destroyed the Temple in 70 A.D. under Titus, seeming to identify the Antichrist as a Roman head of the revived Roman Empire.

That man of sin (2 Thessalonians 2:3). The Antichrist is a lawless individual, the very embodiment of sin.

The son of perdition (2 Thessalonians 2:3). Not only does the Antichrist seek the destruction of others, but it is his own destiny. He is devoted to perdition for others, yet cannot escape it himself.

That wicked one (2 Thessalonians 2:8). Wicked is simply another form of the above mentioned title, "the man of sin." It is his proper name.

The beast ... out of the sea (Revelation 13:1). This name describes both his character and his origin. He is a beast of prey like the one who empowers him (1 Peter 5:8). The sea is thought to be the sea of troubled nations (Isaiah 57:20).

(See also The Beast, 666)

ANTICHRIST, SPIRIT OF

Denial of Jesus Christ is the principle motivating all the antichrists throughout history (1 John 4:3; 2 John 7). This spirit of Antichrist is even now already at work in the world and will culminate in *the* Antichrist being revealed during the Tribulation (1 John 2:18).

In his book *Things to Come*, Dr. J. Dwight Pentecost explains the relation of Antichrist to the two beasts:

The word "antichrist" appears only in the Epistles of John. It is used in 1 John 2:18,22; 4:3, and 2 John 7. A study of these references will reveal that John is principally concerned with an immediate doctrinal error — the denial of the person of Christ. The emphasis is not on a future revelation of an individual, but rather on the present manifestation of false doctrine. To John, Antichrist was already present. The question arises then as to the relation between the "antichrist" of John's epistle and the Beasts of Revelation.

The prefix *anti* may be used either in the sense of "instead of" or "against." Aldrich correctly observes: "The solution of the problem of the identification of Antichrist would seem to depend upon whether light can be thrown on the question of whether he is primarily the great enemy of Christ or whether he is a false Christ."

That these possibilities exist is substantiated by Thayer, who says that the preposition has two primary usages: first, over against or opposite to; and second, indicating an exchange, instead of or in place of. A study of the five usages of "antichrist" in John's epistles seems clearly to indicate the idea of opposition rather than exchange. Trench observes: "To me St. John's words seem decisive that resistance to Christ, and defiance of Him, this, and not any treacherous assumption of his character of offices, is the essential mark of the Anti-christ [sic]; is that which, therefore, we should expect to find embodied in his name . . . and in this sense, if not all, yet many of the Fathers have understood the

word."

The word antichrist seems to be contrasted with "false Christ" in Scripture. This word is used in Matthew 24:24 and Mark 13:22. On the contrast between the words the same author says: "The [Pseudochristos, false Christ] does not deny the being of a Christ; on the contrary, he builds on the world's expectations of such a person; only he appropriates these to himself, blasphemously affirms that he is the foretold One, in whom God's promises and men's expectations are fulfilled . . . ."

The distinction, then, is plain . . . [antichristos, antichrist] denies that there is a Christ; . . . [pseudochristos, false Christ] affirms himself to be Christ.

It would seem that John has the idea of opposition in mind rather than the idea of exchange. This idea of direct opposition to Christ seems to be the particular characterization of the first beast, for he sets his kingdom against the kingdom of the Son of God. If the Antichrist must be identified with one of the two beasts, it would seem to be identified with the first. It may be, however, that John is not referring to either of the two beasts, but rather to the lawless system that will characterize them (2 Thessalonians 2:7). Since he is emphasizing the danger of a present doctrinal defection, he is reminding them that such teaching is the teaching of the antichrist philosophy of Satan that Paul held was already working (2 Thessalonians 2:7).

(See also Mystery of Iniquity)

ANTIOCHUS EPIPHANES

Antiochus IV (c. 215-164 B.C.), was a ruler of the Selucids from 175-164 B.C. and called Epimanes by the Jews, a title of contempt meaning "the madman" (Daniel 8:9-14; 11:21-34).

To antagonize the Jews, he ordered a bearded image of a pagan god to be placed in the Temple. Heathen rites were performed in the Temple and swine were sacrificed on the altar, desecrating it. He is a type of the Antichrist, who behaves in a similar manner during the

Tribulation. He is also called *Little Horn* in Daniel 8:9 (see Abomination of Desolation).

APOCALYPSE

Revelation: something revealed (see Coming of Christ).

APOKALUPSIS (See Christ, Coming of)

APOSTASY

The word apostasy does not appear in the King James Version and the Greek word, *apostasia*, occurs only in 2 Thessalonians 2:3 ("falling away") and Acts 21:21 ("to forsake"); however, the concept occurs often. Another meaning suggested is "withdrawal" or "departure." If this interpretation could be substantiated, it would be another strong argument for the pre-tribulation Rapture view. However, the usual translation (falling away) indicates this to be a time of departure from the faith (2 Thessalonians 2:3) and rebellion against God (1 Timothy 4:1-3; 2 Timothy 4:1).

The Bible teaches that apostates will arise within the Christian church (Acts 20:29; 2 Peter 2:1; Jude 4). They creep in secretly, quietly, and slowly, and once they are in they take over and deny the Lord Jesus Christ. This has to do with His deity (1 Timothy 3:16), His virgin birth (Matthew 1:23), His substitutionary blood atonement (Acts 20:28; Ephesians 1:7). His bodily resurrection (Romans 4:25; 10:9,10), and His bodily return (John 14:1-6; 1 Thessalonians 4:16-18).

The Bible describes the great damage apostates do. In Acts 20:29, they *spare not the flock* (God's people). Romans 16:17,18 says they cause divisions and offenses and deceive simple hearts. In 1 Timothy 4:2 they speak lies in hypocrisy. In 1 Timothy 6:3 they *consent not to wholesome words, even the words of our Lord Jesus Christ.* They overthrow the faith of some (2 Timothy 2:18), bring in *damnable heresies* (2 Peter 2:1), *speak evil of dignities* and *things that they understand not* (2

A APOSTASY

Peter 2:10,12). In 2 Peter 2:14 they have *eyes full of adultery, and that cannot cease from sin*, they also (beguile) unstable souls and *have forsaken the way* and *speak great swelling words of vanity.* Second John 7 says they *confess not that Jesus Christ is come in the flesh* and Jude 4 says they turn *the grace of our God into lasciviousness and* [deny] *the Lord Jesus Christ.* Even if a man who says such things has a doctorate in religion, flee from him!

Consider the names and titles God gives to apostates in inspired scripture: "grievous wolves" (Acts 20:29), "unbelievers" (2 Corinthians 6:14), "false apostles" and "deceitful workers" (2 Corinthians 11:13), "enemies of the cross of Christ" (Philippians 3:18), "men of corrupt minds and destitute of the truth" (1 Timothy 6:5), "vessels of dishonour" (2 Timothy 2:20), "false teachers" (2 Peter 2:1), "natural brute beasts" (2 Peter 2:12), "servants of corruption" (2 Peter 2:19), and "antichrists" (1 John 2:18).

ARABS

Sons of Ishmael through Abraham and Hagar. The fight started then and will continue when in the coming war with Russia, nearly all the Arab nations will be allies, and their primary purpose will be to take a prey ...Israel. (See Psalm 83: 4-7, Ezekiel 38: 5-7 & Daniel 11:40-45).

ARMAGEDDON

This is the closing battle of three and one-half years of skirmish in the Middle East. It begins with Russia's invasion of Israel after the peace contract of Daniel 9:27 is broken (Ezekiel 38:15,16). Additional participants include the kings under the Antichrist from the West (Daniel 7:24; Revelation 13:1), kings of the East under China (Daniel 11:44; Revelation 16:12), and kings of the south, involving much of Africa (Daniel 11:11).

Miracles performed through satanic power will convince the leaders of the earth, who are subservient to the Antichrist, to move all of their military might to the Middle East to do battle with Christ at His return to the

Mount of Olives (Zechariah 14:4; Revelation 16:14).

They will not be disappointed: Christ will come. The Battle of Armageddon climaxes the campaign as the Lord and His armies appear from heaven. The armies of earth will march to their doom, expecting to destroy the Christ they have rejected (Joel 3:9-14; Psalm 2:2,3); Revelation 19:11-21). Christ, the living Word of God returns, riding on a white horse. His eyes are as a flame of fire and his vesture dipped in blood bears the name, King of Kings and Lord of Lords. Followed by the armies of heaven, He will smite the nations and cause the Beast and the False Prophet to be cast into the Lake of Fire.

It will be the bloodiest battle in the history of the world. Militarists from the four corners of the earth will battle Almighty God and the hosts of heaven (Psalm 2:2; Isaiah 34:2; Zechariah 14:3; Revelation 9:16) will engage in the earth's greatest power struggle. So great will be the destruction resulting that the blood will reach to the horse's bridles for 200 miles and it will require mankind seven months to bury the dead (Revelation 14:20; Ezekiel 39:12).

ASTROLOGY

The Antichrist will be associated with astrology and witchcraft (Daniel 8:23).

ATOMIC WAR (See Nuclear War, Days of Lot, Signs, America)

AUTOMOBILES (See Signs)

BEAST OUT OF THE SEA **B**

BABYLON

God's Word mentions three Babylons: a city (Genesis 11), a church (Revelation 17), and a country (Revelation 18). Don't confuse the three by intermingling these chapters. The context of each text identifies who is who.

The ancient city, Babylon, was built by Nimrod (Genesis 10:10), came into its greatest power under Nebuchadnezzar (Daniel 4:30), was the scene of Jewish captivity (2 Kings 25:1-21; 2 Chronicles 36:5-21; Acts 7:43), fell (Isaiah 13:1-22; Jeremiah 50:1-46), and was destined for perpetual desolation (Isaiah 13:19-22; Jeremiah 50:13,39).

The false church, Mystery Babylon the Great, is called the Mother of Harlots, (Revelation 17:3-5). Spiritual fornication in Scripture has reference to adherence to a false system. In contrast to the true Church, the "Bride of Christ," this system has fallen from its pure position and become a harlot. This "great whore" (Revelation 17:1) is located in Rome, the eternal city, situated geographically upon seven hills (17:9), reigning over the kings of the earth (17:18). It is likely that the gloriously revived Roman Empire will bring this united world church into prominence. It is seen to be controlling the Beast upon which it sits. This system will be destroyed by the Beast so that his supremacy may not be threatened (Revelation 17:16,17) (see Woman).

The country, political Babylon (Isaiah 50,51), is probably the United States of America (see America).

BEAST, THE

The rise of the Antichrist, the Beast, is the most significant political event during the Tribulation period. He is described by John in Revelation 13. Daniel spoke of him as the "little horn" whose power would reach its zenith for three and one-half years (Daniel 7:8; 8:9). He will control the economies of the world.
(See also Antichrist, 666)

BEAST OUT OF THE SEA (See Antichrist)

B BEASTS, FOUR

BEASTS, FOUR (of Revelation 4)

These are literal, created beings connected with the throne room of heaven (Revelation 4:6). They have eyes before and behind to see all things clearly and accurately (Revelation 4:6). By comparing the characteristics of these living creatures with Isaiah 6:1-3, we see that they are undoubtedly seraphim — angels of God — created to praise and exalt the Lord. These beings are not monstrosities. Instead, they are a picture of beauty. This is a portrait set before us . . . angels in all their magnificence praising the Lord.

BEASTS, FOUR (of Daniel 7)

The Prophet Daniel interpreted Nebuchadnezzar's dream when he was a very young man. Nearly 40 years later he was given a vision that confirmed and further explained his first preview of the future. In this vision Daniel saw the major world empires represented by four beasts:

1. The lion represents Nebuchadnezzar's Babylonian Empire.

2. The bear is the Medo-Persian Empire that followed. (The bear was raised on one side because the Persians were stronger than the Medes. The three ribs in the bear's mouth indicate three major conquests.)

3. The leopard, having four wings and four heads, was a prophetic picture of the Grecian Empire. (After the death of Alexander the Great, his empire was divided between his four generals.)

4. The fourth beast, described as "dreadful and terrible," and "strong exceedingly," represents the Roman Empire. His ten horns, which correspond to the ten toes on the image, represent ten nations that once were part of the Roman Empire. The "little horn speaking great things" will emerge as a powerful political leader to whom three national heads will give their full allegiance . . . the Antichrist.

BEGINNING OF SORROWS (See Sorrow)

BEMA (See Judgment Seat of Christ)

BINDING OF SATAN

Satan, as the god of this age (2 Corinthians 4:4), has worked tirelessly to defeat the purpose and plan of God. The millennial age will be an age in which divine righteousness is enforced as Christ rules with a rod of iron (Isaiah 11:5; 32:1; Jeremiah 23:6; Daniel 9:24; Revelation 19:15). It is also to be God's final test of fallen humanity under ideal circumstances. All outward sources of temptation must be removed so that man will demonstrate what he is apart from satanic influence. Therefore, Satan must be bound and removed for the entire millennial period. After the thousand-year reign, he is loosed and multitudes once again follow him. How wicked the human heart is (Revelation 20:7,8).

BLASPHEMY (See Signs)

BLESSED HOPE (See Second Coming of Christ)

BLINDNESS, ISRAEL

The New Testament teaches that the nation of Israel is presently blinded. Not only are they spiritually blind because they willfully reject their Messiah, but a divine judgment has come upon them so that the nation is also judicially blinded (Isaiah 6:9,10; Matthew 13:14,15; Mark 4:12; Luke 8:10; John 12:40; Acts 28:26,27). It is a continuing state (2 Corinthians 3:14,15), yet, one day the veil over their hearts shall be taken away (vs. 16). The longest passage dealing with the subject is found in Romans 11:17-27. This passage reveals five factors concerning Israel's blindness:

1. *It is a mystery.* A mystery refers to some divine program that could not and would not have been known unless it had been revealed to men by God. It is different from the spiritual blindness all originally inherit as children of Adam under the curse of sin. This is willful

blindness as a result of Israel's sinning against revealed light, rejecting the Messiah (Matthew 27:25).

2. *The nature of this blindness* is revealed from the word *porosis* which literally means "to harden by covering with a callus because of repeated rejection of the revelation that was given."

3. *The blindness is in part.* It is not universal so there is the possibility of an individual's salvation even though the nation has been judicially blinded.

4. There is a definite time when *the blindness will be removed from the nation.*

5. *The time of removal* is stated, "until the fullness of the Gentiles be come in" (see Gentiles, Fullness of). Remember that removal of the national blindness does not mean the clear revelation of spiritual truth to the individual Jew. He still possesses the blindness of his sin nature. The removal of the judicial blindness permits Israel to hear the good news of the kingdom (Matthew 24:14) in order that they might be saved, both individually and nationally . . . making possible the choosing and calling of the 144,000, the calling out of the believing remnant, and Israel's ministry to the nations during the Tribulation period.

BLOOD

Bloodshed is evidenced everywhere in the violence of the Tribulation Hour culminating in Armageddon. Yet, even then, another form of blood-shedding, remembering Calvary and the cross, brings victory (Revelation 12:13). John the Baptist said, *Behold the Lamb of God, which taketh away the sin of the world* (John 1:29). Salvation came by the shedding of Christ's blood in John's day as he looked ahead to the Crucifixion. It also does now and during the coming Tribulation by remembering Calvary. The 144,000 will preach the same message as John: "The King is coming! Repent and trust in the sacrifice of the Lamb of God." Remember, *without shedding of blood, there is no remission* (Hebrews 9:22; Revelation 7:14). Those martyred, because of their faith in Christ's

sacrifice during the awful days of the Tribulation, are referred to as *they which came out of great tribulation, and have washed their robes, and made them white in the blood of the Lamb* (Revelation 7:14).
(See Gospel of the Kingdom)

BODIES, GLORIFIED AND NATURAL
Glorified

The risen Saviour had a glorified (resurrection) body of flesh and bones, one that could be seen, touched, and fed. Glorified bodies will have the same supernatural qualities as Christ's had (passing through walls, instantaneous travel) (Luke 24:36-51; 1 John 3:2). The only way to obtain a glorified body is through resurrection and rapture.

When a believer dies, his spirit and soul go into the presence of God, but his body goes into the grave (2 Corinthians 5:8). His soul, absent from the body, is with Christ until the great day when body, soul, and spirit are reunited at the coming of Jesus (1 Thessalonians 4:16-18) (see Rapture). Christ will bring the souls and spirits of the dead in Christ with Him (vs. 14) to be reunited with their vacated bodies when He returns at the Rapture. All believers, first the dead, then the living, will join Him bodily in the clouds. The bodies, dead and living, that rise for this reunion will be transformed to be like Jesus' body (1 John 3:2; Psalm 17:15; 1 Corinthians 15:51-54; Philippians 3:20,21). Even though many may have completely disintegrated to basic chemical makeup, God is able to restore (He created Adam from dust. Science tells us that matter never completely disappears, only changes form.)

Natural

Our natural bodies are essentially the same as when God created Adam and Eve in Eden but they are fatally altered because of Adam's fall. Mankind was meant to eternally fellowship with and glorify Him who created us for that purpose. However, Adam's sin brought death to our natural bodies as well as spiritual death to our

B BODIES, GLORIFIED AND NATURAL

souls. Our bodies deteriorate as they age and eventually die by disease, accident, or just wearing out.

True to the term, Saviour, Jesus Christ rescued us, body and soul, by His death, burial, and resurrection.

1. Our souls can be "born again" (John 3:3,5,7; 1 Corinthians 15:20-23) and continue to fellowship with Him as our physical, temporal bodies become temples of the Holy Spirit here on earth (1 Corinthians 6:19; Revelation 3:20) (see also Temple).

2. Our bodies will be "changed," like unto His resurrected body because He took upon himself the penalty of our sins (death and separation from God), and died and rose again to be the "first-fruits" (1 Corinthians 15:20-23; 2 Corinthians 5:19) (see also Romans 8:23).

The saints who return with Jesus for Armageddon will have their glorified bodies while those who will have survived the Tribulation and have not been condemned in the judgment of the nations (Matthew 25:31-46) are allowed to enter the Millennium in their mortal bodies.

When souls in Hades are resurrected after the Millennium for the day of judgment, they are reunited with their bodies that will suffer physically in the Lake of Fire (Revelation 20:11-15). Yet, they don't die and aren't consumed as the "worm dieth not." What kind of bodies are these resurrection bodies? They surely have special enduring qualities that natural bodies do not have. These bodies can't die because they are "equal to the angels" . . . apparently all resurrection bodies are not glorified bodies (Daniel 12:2; John 5:28,29; Revelation 20:13; Luke 20:36).

Perhaps people who choose for Christ after the Millennium, have some kind of enduring bodies because they ate of the leaves of the trees from the New Jerusalem and therefore their bodies endure forever. After the Millennium, in eternity, the redeemed will continue to inhabit the New Jerusalem in their heavenly bodies. Those with earthly bodies (who were saved for and in the millennial hour) enter the eternal state with their natural bodies. These bodies also will be eternally preserved through partaking of the leaves of the trees of life that grow for the healing (health) of the nations (Revelation 22:2,14). They will live on earth, in and under the light of the Holy City (Revelation 21:24). Their condition will be like that of Adam and Eve before they sinned.

BONES, DRY

A vivid description of the scattering and return of Israel is given by the Prophet Ezekiel in his vision of the valley of dry bones. He is transported to a great valley full of dry, bleached bones exposed to the wind and sun. He was asked if those bones could live and was also told to prophecy about them. While he was speaking, the bones came together and the skeletons, covered with flesh and given life, stood to their feet and became a great army.

The bones represent Israel (Ezekiel 37:11). Their disconnectedness and dryness indicate Israel's scattering and lack of hope. The graves are the nations in which they dwell. The imparting of sinew, flesh, and breath is a miracle timed for the last days.

The Jews are to come out of the nations to which they have been scattered. They will return in unbelief without spiritual life, but finally after being settled in their land, there will come a time of conversion, of new birth (Ezekiel 37:1-14).

BOOK OF LIFE

This is the Book that is opened at the Great White Throne Judgment in which the names of all those who responded to God's call of salvation are written, guaranteeing them a place in heaven. Those not found in this Book are to be cast into the Lake of Fire (Exodus 32:32,33; Psalm 69:28; Luke 10:20; Philippians 4:3; Revelation 3:5; 13:8; 20:12,15; 21:27).

BOOK OF REMEMBRANCE

Another book opened at the Great White Throne

Judgment in which God recorded the deeds of people on earth (Malachi 3:16). These facts will be a source of comfort but also of embarrassment and shame (Daniel 7:10; Revelation 20:12). God knows us very well (Psalm 139:1,2; Ezekiel 11:5; 2 Peter 2:14). He knows our hearts (Jeremiah 17:10; Matthew 15:19). God's books arc totally accurate because He sees every move one makes (2 Chronicles 16:9; Hebrews 4:13).

BOOK, THE

The book is actually a scroll enclosed with seven seals. It is the title deed to the earth and its subject is redemption. The Lamb of God (John 1:29), who earned the right by redemption, is the only One worthy to open the seals on the book.

BOOK, THE LITTLE

The "little book" that John is commanded to take and eat is either all or a portion of the Word of God dealing with the judgments. The message John is about to share is bittersweet. Devouring God's message of salvation is very sweet (Jeremiah 15:16; Psalm 119:103; Revelation 10:10). Yet, as it is assimilated and judgments are experienced, it becomes bitter.

BOTTOMLESS PIT

This term, (Greek rendering, "pit of the abyss") is found nine times in the New Testament. In each case it is a place to restrain or hold certain beings which have come under the judgment of God (Luke 8:31). It will be the holding place of Satan during the Millennium (Revelation 20:1-3).

BOWLS (also referred to as vials)

A total of 21 judgments are unleashed upon the earth during the Tribulation Hour. The bowls contain seven of these (Revelation 16) (see also Judgments).

BRIDE OF CHRIST

The Church (all born-again believers collectively) is represented as a chaste virgin (2 Corinthians 11:2). According to marriage customs explained in biblical texts, the Church (the Bride), is now in the betrothal stage, promised to Jesus Christ. As His fianceé, He wants us to live holy lives. The Church, or Bride, is to be clothed in fine, white linen (Revelation 19:7,8). Her wedding gown will actually be composed of righteous deeds she (the believers) performed while on earth.

Her wedding takes place in heaven, but the Marriage Supper occurs on earth. At the hour when Christ returns to earth with His Bride, a 1,000-year honeymoon begins (see also Judgment Seat of Christ, Marriage Supper of the Lamb, and Millennium).

BRIDEGROOM

The Lord Jesus himself is the Bridegroom (Ephesians 5:25-33).

CHARIOTS (See Automobiles)

CHRIST, COMING OF

Several terms occur in Scripture which refer to the coming of Christ. It is important to know how these words are used in order that we might have a more accurate understanding of Scripture and prophecy in particular. None of these terms is used exclusively for any one appearing of Christ. Each term has more than one usage.

Appearance: "a shining forth" used only for appearances of Christ at the Incarnation (2 Timothy 1:10), at the Rapture (1 Timothy 6:14; 2 Timothy 4:1,8; Titus 2:13), or at the Second Advent (His "revealing to earth" or revelation) (2 Thessalonians 2:8).

Epiphany: comes from the Greek word, *epiphaneia*, used extensively in the New Testament to denote a coming of Christ (1 Timothy 1:15; John 14:3; Matthew 24:30).

Presence (*parousia*): emphasizes the bodily presence rather than the act of coming (2 Corinthians 10:10; Philippians 2:12 . . . lit.).

Revelation (*apokalupsis*): "to uncover, unveil, to reveal" the future manifestation of Christ (1 Corinthians 1:7; 1 Peter 1:7; Luke 17:30; 2 Thessalonians 1:7).

CHRIST, MILLENNIAL NAMES AND TITLES

The multiple relationships of Christ in the Millennium are manifested in the many names and titles given Him describing facts about Him and His work in that day.

The Branch, of Jehovah, (Isaiah 4:2); of David, (Jeremiah 23:5; 33:15); Jehovah's Servant, the Branch (Zechariah 3:8); the man whose name is the Branch, (Zechariah 6:12,13).

Names showing that the One ruling is truly God:
ANCIENT OF DAYS (Daniel 7:13)

C CHRIST, MILLENNIAL NAMES AND TITLES

JEHOVAH (Isaiah 2:2-4; 7:14; 9:6; 12:6; 25:7-10; 33:20-22; 40:9-11; Jeremiah 3:17; 23:5,6; Ezekiel 43:5-7; 44:1,2; Joel 3:21; Micah 4:1-3,7; Zechariah 14:9,16,17)

THE LORD OF HOSTS (Isaiah 24:23; 46:6)

THE LORD OUR RIGHTEOUSNESS (Jeremiah 23:6; 33:16)

THE LORD (Micah 4:7; Zechariah 14:9)

THE MOST HIGH (Daniel 7:22-24)

SON OF GOD (Isaiah 9:6; Daniel 3:25; Hosea 11:1)

THY GOD (Isaiah 53:7)

Names showing His humanity:
ROD OF JESSE (Isaiah 11:1,11)

SERVANT (Isaiah 42:1-6; 49:1-7; 53:11)

SON OF MAN (Daniel 7:13)

TENDER PLANT (Isaiah 53:2; Ezekiel 17:22-24)

Names showing His regal authority:
JUDGE (Isaiah 11:3,4; 16:5; 33:22; 51:4,5; Ezekiel 34:17,20; Joel 3:1,2; Micah 4:2,3)

KING (Isaiah 2:2-4; 9:3-7; 11:1-10; 16:5; 24:21; 26:15; 31:4; 32:2; 33:17,22; 42:13; 44:6; 49:1-9; 51:4,5; 60:12; Daniel 2:44; 7:15-28; Obadiah 17:21; Micah 4:1-8; 5:2-5,15; Zechariah 3:9,10,18,19; Zechariah 9:10-15; 14:16,17)

LAWGIVER (Isaiah 33:22)

MESSIAH, THE PRINCE (Daniel 9:25,26)

PRINCE OF PRINCES (Daniel 8:25)

Names showing the work of the King as Redeemer in bringing salvation:
LIGHT (Isaiah 60:1-3)

LORD OF RIGHTEOUSNESS (Jeremiah 23:6; 33:16)

REDEEMER (Isaiah 59:20)

SHEPHERD (Isaiah 40:10,11; Jeremiah 23:1,3; Ezekiel 34:11-31; 37:24; Micah 4:5; 7:14)

STONE (Isaiah 28:16; Zechariah 3:9)

SUN OF RIGHTEOUSNESS (Malachi 4:2)

WALL BREAKER (Micah 2:13)

CHRIST, PROPHECIES FULFILLED

1. He would be the seed of a woman (Genesis 3:15).
2. He would come through the line of Abraham, Isaac, and Jacob (Genesis 12:3,17-19).
3. He would be a descendant of Judah (Genesis 49:10).
4. He would be born in Bethlehem (Micah 5:2).
5. He would be born of a virgin (Isaiah 7:14).
6. He would sojourn into Egypt (Hosea 11:1).
7. He would grow up at Nazareth and be called a Nazarene (Matthew 22:14-16).
8. He would be crucified (Psalm 22:14-16)
9. He would suffer no broken bones at His crucifixion (Psalm 34:20).
10. He would observe men casting lots for His clothing at His crucifixion (Psalm 34:20).
11. He would live again (Job 19:25; Matthew 12:39,40; 16:3; John 2:19). Both recorded history and fulfilled prophecy prove that each point came to pass.

CHRISTOPHANY (See Angels)

CHRONOLOGY

The Book of Revelation is presented in chronological order (Revelation 1:19). Notice the sequence: past — *write the things which thou hast seen* (chapter 1), present — *write the things which are* (chapters 2 and 3), and future — *write the things which shall be* (chapters 4-22).

In chapters 2 and 3, the panoramic historical view of the seven churches is presented. The churches of Philadelphia and Laodicia are both present in modern Christendom. Some portray the Laodician church as merely professing Christians (Titus 1:15) while others believe they are simply lukewarm, lazy Christians who meet Christ "ashamed" (Revelation 3:16; 1 John 2:28). The church of Philadelphia is snatched away before the judgments begin (Revelation 6). The church is conspicuously absent after chapter 4 . . . a proof of a pre-tribulational Rapture.

In Revelation 4:1, we find that, "after this" (the events of chapters 2 and 3), a door opens in heaven and a voice (like a trumpet) calls, "Come up hither . . . ." This is the Rapture, the snatching away (1 Corinthians 15:51-55), the call of the Bridegroom for His Bride.

The Bride (the Church) is then carried to heaven where the Judgment Seat of Christ takes place and the marriage of the Lamb occurs (Revelation 19:7,8). This will transpire simultaneously with the Tribulation on earth (2 Corinthians 5:10; Romans 14:10; 1 Corinthians 3:11-15; Revelation 3:10).

The Tribulation, depicted in Revelation 6, begins after the Rapture and continues until the Battle of Armageddon when Christ returns as King of Kings and Lord of Lords to fight the armies of the world (Revelation 19:11-16). Christ brings His Bride back with Him for this battle (Revelation 19:14).

After Christ's victory, pre- and post-Grace Age saints are raised (Daniel 12:2). They, like John the Baptist, are not part of the Bride, but friends of Christ, the Bridegroom. Their resurrection is at the conclusion of the Tribulation and they are present at the Marriage Supper which takes place on earth soon after (see Marriage Supper of the Lamb).

There is a further division to be made in order to make the Book of Revelation perfectly clear. Chapters 4-11 picture the seven-year Tribulation and chapter 11 portrays the return of Christ to earth (vs. 15-18). Chapters 12 to 19 depict the identical scene a second time and Christ's return is again described in verse 11 of chapter 19.

Apparently there will be a 75-day interval of transition between Christ's return and the beginning of the Millennium (Daniel 12:11,12). During this time Christ destroys the world's armies (Revelation 19:14,15; Isaiah 34:1-3), regathers Israel (Isaiah 43:5,6; Ezekiel 36:28; Matthew 24:31), separates the sheep nations from the goat nations (Matthew 25:31-46), binds Satan (Revelation 19:20; Revelation 20:1-3), resurrects the Old Testament and Tribulation saints (Job 19:25,26; Isaiah 25:8; 26:19; Daniel 12:2; Revelation 20:4,5), and judges the fallen angels (1 Corinthians 6:3). (If those saints have to be at the Marriage Supper, then perhaps the Marriage Supper takes place during this interval???)

Next comes the Millennium, 1,000 years of peace (Revelation 20). Then, after ten glorious centuries, Satan is loosed for a season allowing those born during that era to choose for or against Christ. Many rebel and follow Satan and are cast with him into the Lake of Fire (Revelation 20:9,10).

Following this is the Great White Throne Judgment for the resurrected unbelievers of all ages (Revelation 20:11-15). Finally the present earth and heavens are destroyed (2 Peter 3:10,11; Matthew 24:35; Isaiah 48:10) and God creates a new heaven and a new earth (Isaiah 65:17; Revelation 21:2,10). *Even so, come, Lord Jesus* (Revelation 22:20).

CHURCH, THE

The Church is comprised of all born-again believers in Christ as Saviour, both Jew and Gentile, from Pentecost until the Rapture (Ephesians 2:13-15). We become one in Christ at conversion (1 Corinthians 12:13). We are presently living in the Church Age or Age of Grace and this will continue until the Rapture.

CHURCH AGE (Parenthetical Period)

For nearly 2,000 years we have been living in a parenthesis, a prophetic interval.

Daniel's prophecy in the vision of the 70 weeks (or 70 seven-year periods) called for a total of 490 years when God would deal especially with Israel. When Christ offered himself as the Prince of Israel, 483 years, or 69 weeks of years had been fulfilled. When He was rejected and crucified, the prophetic clock stopped, not to begin again until the Jews were back in their land and the parenthetical period had ended.

During this interval, sometimes known as the Church Age, or Age of Grace, both Jews and Gentiles who are born again through faith in Christ become part of the body of Christ or the Bride of Christ. The signal that the "in between" period has ended, will be the removal of the Church (the Bride of Christ) from the earth. This great event is described in a number of Bible texts. One of the clearest is 1 Thessalonians 4:13-18. Then the prophetical clock ticks again for the final (70th) week. In addition, Dr. Dwight Pentecost says:

When the Lord returns with His bride to reign, her dwelling place is not to be left unoccupied for a thousand years. Rather, the place of occupancy is transferred from heaven to a position over the earth. Thus, John sees the "great city" descending out of heaven from God. This dwelling place remains in the air to cast its light . . . on the earth so that *the nations of them which are saved shall walk in the light of it; and the kings of the earth do bring their glory and honour unto it* (Revelation 21:24). At the second advent, the time of the descent of the city into the air over the earth, the church saints are joined by the Old Testament saints, who are resurrected and take up residence at that time.

It may thus be seen that even though the earth is not in its eternal state, and though it is necessary for the King to rule the earth with a rod of iron, and though there will be a rebellion against the authority of the King, yet, as far as the church is concerned, she is in her eternal state, enjoying her eternal fellowship, and the fruits of her salvation. From that heavenly city she will reign with Him, the One who bears the title of King of Kings and Lord of Lords. It is not eternity, but the church and the redeemed of the ages are in their eternal state.

Then he quotes Kelly:

There are two descents of the city in chapter 21,

one at the beginning of the Millennium, and the other at the commencement of the eternal state. The second verse of that chapter gives us its descent when the eternal state is come, and the tenth verse its descent for the Millennium. The reason, I think, is that at the end of the Millennium the old heaven and earth pass away; and naturally the city would disappear from the scene of the convulsion. Then, when the new earth dawns on our view, the heavenly city again comes down and takes its place permanently in the new heavens and earth (while at the end of the thousand years all will be changed, still the heavenly city will abide forever) (see also Rapture).

CHURCHES, SEVEN

The letters to the seven churches may have a number of applications. First, they are sent to seven literal, local churches (Revelation 1:11). Second, they are letters to seven individuals within the churches. Third, they are messages applicable to all churches in all ages, for they picture seven periods or stages of church history. The following is a list of these churches (church ages also) and their main weakness (the Lord begins by commending each assembly for whatever good He can find in them before scolding them):

1. Ephesus — lax in their judgment of False Prophets
2. Smyrna — fearful
3. Pergamos — became worldly and embraced false doctrines
4. Thyatira — followed the teachings of Jezebel
5. Sardis — dead orthodoxy
6. Philadelphia — warned to be faithful or lose their reward
7. Laodiceans — lukewarm

CLOTHING

Clothing seems to signify either position or condition. The false church, the Mother of Harlots, wore purple

C CLOTHING

and scarlet signifying her filthiness through fornication (Revelation 17:4).

The angels in Revelation 15:6, dressed the same as the Old Testament priests, ministering in pure white linen and golden girdles . . . as Christ, our High Priest, pictured holiness.

The two witnesses wore sackcloth, which has always pictured repentance (Revelation 11).

White raiment is found upon the Bride of Christ signifying her righteousness (Revelation 19:7,8).

The Laodiceans were told to get white clothes, a symbol of righteousness, to cover their shameful nakedness or wicked ways.

White signifies purity. The overcomers who did not defile their garments will walk with Christ in white (Revelation 3:4), along with the Tribulation saints who have washed their robes and made them white in the blood of the Lamb (Revelation 7:14).

COMMON MARKET NATIONS (See Roman Empire, Revived, Ten Nation Confederacy)

COMMUNISM (See Russia)

COMPUTERS (See Image of the Beast, 666)

CORRUPTION (See Signs)

COVENANT

A divinely initiated contract which God makes with man in which God obligates himself to the parties named in the contract. A covenant may be unconditional (God says, "I will . . ."), or conditional (God says, "I will, if you will . . ."). It is important to note the difference. J. Dwight Pentecost says, "The covenants contained in the Scriptures are of primary importance to the interpreter of the Word and to the student of Eschatology. God's eschatological program is determined and prescribed by these covenants and one's eschatological system is determined and limited by the interpretation of them. These covenants must be studied diligently as the basis of Biblical Eschatology." His book, *Things to Come*, covers the covenants in depth and I encourage you to study it for detailed information.

The following is an outline of the major covenants having to do with prophetic truth:

ABRAHAMIC COVENANT

This is the foundation of all the succeeding covenants to Israel in which God promises unconditionally to raise up a seed unto Abraham and to give him and his seed an everlasting possession (Genesis 12:1-3; 13:14-18; 15:1-21; 17:1-22). In this covenant, God promises:

1. To make of Abraham a great nation, to multiply his seed exceedingly and to make him a father of many nations
2. To bless Abraham and make him great
3. To make Abraham a blessing to all the families of the earth
4. To bless those who bless him and curse those who curse him
5. To give Abraham and his seed forever all the land which he could see, later specified with definite boundaries
6. To give him a sign of the covenant (circumcision)

This covenant is partially fulfilled and will not be fully realized until Israel enters into the millennial kingdom.

MOSAIC COVENANT

This covenant with Israel was conditioned upon their obedience to God's commands (Exodus 19:4-6).

In this covenant, God promises:

1. To make Israel His special possession among the people of the land
2. To make Israel a kingdom of priests and a holy nation

God followed it up with requirements and laws.

C COVENANT

Although Israel said, "All that the Lord hath spoken we will do," they soon forgot their promise. This covenant did not supersede the Abrahamic Covenant (Galatians 3:17,18) and even though Israel failed to heed God's commands, the promises of the unconditional, eternal covenant to Abraham were still in force.

PALESTINIAN COVENANT

An unconditional covenant enlarging upon the Abrahamic Covenant promising the seed of Abraham eternal possession in the land (Deuteronomy 30:1-10).

This covenant says:
1. Israel will be dispersed among the nations
2. Israel will repent and turn to the Lord
3. Israel will be regathered from its dispersion

In this covenant, God promises:'
1. To bring them to the land which their fathers possessed
2. To prosper them above their fathers
3. To restore them spiritually so that Israel will love the Lord with all their heart and soul
4. To put all the curses upon their enemies

Pentecost maintains: "It should be observed that the only conditional element here is the time element. The program is certain; the time when this program will be fulfilled depends upon the conversion of the nation. Conditional time elements do not make the whole program conditional, however."

DAVIDIC COVENANT

An unconditional covenant which God made with David reaffirming the Abrahamic Covenant and adding that the blessings would be attached to the lineage of David (2 Samuel 7:1-16; 23:1-5; Psalm 89:34-37).

In this covenant, God promises:
1. To make David's name great
2. To provide a permanent, undisturbed home for Israel
3. To establish an eternal kingdom with David and

his offspring

NEW COVENANT

An unconditional covenant God made with Israel to replace the Mosaic Covenant which the people had failed to obey. He promises Israel a spiritual restoration (Jeremiah 31:31-40).

In this covenant, God promises:

1. To put His law in their hearts and minds
2. To be their God and make them His people
3. To forgive their wickedness and not remember their sins any more

The moral problem posed by the failure of the Mosaic Covenant will, under the new covenant, be met by God's own sovereign grace and power. It is in the gracious spirit of the earlier Abrahamic Covenant, rather than in the legalistic spirit of the Mosaic Covenant which it replaces.

COVETOUS (See Signs)

CROWNS (See Rewards, Judgment Seat of Christ)

DANIEL'S VISION OF SEVENTY WEEKS **D**

DANIEL'S VISION OF SEVENTY WEEKS

Skeptics dislike the Prophet Daniel. His outline of the future is too accurate. By interpreting King Nebuchadnezzar's dream as a young man, he gave us what has come to be known as the "ABC's of Prophecy" (see Nebuchadnezzar's Dream).

Near the end of his life, Daniel was visited by the angel Gabriel and he was given a timetable of coming events that would especially affect Israel. This is known as the Vision of Seventy Weeks. It may well be that this vision is the backbone of prophecy. In this vision Daniel saw the major world empires represented by four beasts (Daniel 7).

The first beast was like a lion, and it had eagle's wings (7:4).

The second beast was like a bear that raised itself on one side having three ribs in its mouth (7:5).

The third was like a leopard, having four wings and four heads (7:6).

The fourth was described as *dreadful and terrible, and strong exceedingly*. It had ten horns and after a time another little horn grew and plucked up three of the other horns by the roots. The little horn had eyes like a man and a mouth speaking great things (7:7,8).

What do these four beasts signify? Currently, the lion with eagle's wings could be the British Empire and the United States. The bear could be Russia and the leopard symbolizes the African nations, since that area is the leopard's natural home. The fourth beast, exceedingly strong, could be the revived Roman Empire (see the Ten Nation Conspiracy).

Historically, students of Bible prophecy have seen the vision as a further development of the preview given in Nebuchadnezzar's dream . . . the context demands it.

The lion represents Nebuchadnezzar's Babylonian Empire.

The bear is the Medo-Persian Empire that followed. It was raised on one side because the Persians were stronger than the Medes. The three ribs indicate their conquests.

The leopard, with four wings and four heads, was a picture of the Grecian Empire. Alexander the Great died and his empire was divided between his four generals.

The fourth beast, described as *dreadful and terrible, and strong exceedingly* represents the Roman Empire.

The prophet is fascinated by the ten horns, which correspond to the ten toes on the image and especially by the little horn that rises later, portraying a powerful leader in the endtime (Daniel 7:24,25).

This mathematical revelation gave the Jews the exact time to expect the coming of their Messiah. It also prophesied His death and foretold the coming destruction of Jerusalem following His crucifixion, as well as the rise of the Antichrist and the establishment of Christ's coming kingdom on earth (Daniel 9:24-27).

The seventy weeks are weeks of years (70 x 7 = 490). This period of time is divided into three sections. The first division comprised seven weeks or a period of 49 years and had to do with the rebuilding of Jerusalem (Daniel 9:25). The second division of 62 weeks, or 434 years, signaled the time of Christ's death after the rebuilding of Jerusalem. Christ came on schedule and was rejected (cut off, vs. 26) resulting in the Crucifixion. Now Israel must pay the price for rejecting her King. So a final week is coming when the Antichrist will confirm his peace covenant for one week, or seven years (vs. 27). This harmonizes with the calculations of the second half of the Tribulation Hour described as a period of "forty-two months" (Revelation 11:2) or 1,260 days (Revelation 11:3), when the Antichrist breaks all of his pledges to Israel and an era of unthinkable persecution breaks out for the Jews especially. Between the weeks 69 and 70 is a parenthesis, unseen in Old Testament prophecy, which applies to the present age (see Tribulation, Jacob's Trouble, Antichrist).

DAVID, KING (See Government of Millennium)

DAY

The word "day" is used many ways in Scripture:
1. A 24-hour day
2. Daytime . . . that part of the day that is light (Psalm 22:2)
3. A period of time (2 Corinthians 6:2)

DAY OF CHRIST

The special day in the life of our Lord when He comes for His Bride is called the Rapture (Philippians 1:10; 2:16). It is also called *the Day of the Lord Jesus Christ* (1 Corinthians 1:8), *the Day of the Lord Jesus* (1 Corinthians 5:5; 2 Corinthians 1:14), *the day of Jesus Christ* (Philippians 1:6).

This term should not be confused with "the Day of the Lord." Note that the term "day of Christ" in 2 Thessalonians 2:2 should be translated "Day of the Lord."

DAY OF ETERNITY

The beginning of the eternal state, the same as the day of God (2 Peter 3:18) . . . that wondrous day when He shall return shall usher in eternity for the universe.

DAY OF GOD

(2 Peter 3:12) (See Day of Eternity)

DAY OF THE LORD

The Day of the Lord begins as the Tribulation period commences. It continues through the 1,000-year reign of Christ because the destruction of the world by fire afterward is still called the Day of the Lord (2 Peter 3:10). Some try to make this the Rapture causing confusion. It begins immediately *after* the Rapture. This is the reason that the Day of the Lord comes as *a thief in the night* (1 Thessalonians 5:2).

DAY OF REDEMPTION

The day when Christ returns for His saints at the Rapture and gives His redeemed their new glorified bodies (Ephesians 1:14; Romans 8:23). The deliverance from the effects of sin will be completed. All believers are sealed by the Holy Spirit until the day of redemption, or the Rapture (Ephesians 4:30).

DAYS OF LOT (See Signs, Nuclear War)

DAYS OF NOAH (See Signs)

DEAD SEA (See Russia)

DEATH

Physical death is the separation of the soul from the body, a result of man's sin (Genesis 2:17; Romans 5:11), and the last enemy to be defeated (1 Corinthians 15:26). It is not annihilation. For the believer, death is simply the gateway into the presence of God (2 Corinthians 5:8; Revelation 14:13).

Elijah (2 Kings 2) and Enoch (Genesis 5:22-24) are the only persons to have escaped death up to this time. Believers living at the Rapture will also escape physical death by being translated directly into heaven (1 Thessalonians 4:17).

Spiritual death is separation of the person from God, the condition of every unsaved person, a direct result of the fall of man (Isaiah 59:2; Ephesians 2:1; Colossians 2:13). The believer is freed from spiritual death when he is saved. He is *alive in Christ* (Ephesians 2:5) and is *passed from death unto life* (John 5:24).

The "second death" is eternal separation of the unbeliever from God in the Lake of Fire (Revelation 20:6,14; 21:8). It is everlasting and must not be thought of as annihilation at any point in time or eternity (the Antichrist and the False Prophet are still alive after 1,000 years in the Lake of Fire) (Revelation 19:20; 20:10).

The second death has no hold whatever upon the believer (Revelation 20:6). The hope of the believer is immortality, eternal life, and heaven! Christ, our

Saviour, is the only One with power over death (2 Timothy 1:10).

DEATH, SECOND (See Hell, Lake of Fire)

DEMONS

The world is experiencing initial preparations for a demonic invasion as Satan and his cohorts come to wreak havoc (Revelation 12:9). A description of some of these demons is presented in verses 7 and 8 of Revelation 9 (see signs — Murder, Drug Addiction, Sex, and Burglary).

DIASPORA (See Israel . . . Dispersion)

DISOBEDIENT (See Signs)

DISPENSATIONALISM

A system of theology that, among other things, recognizes three basic tenets:

1. There is a theological distinction between Israel and the Church
2. Scripture is to be interpreted consistently by the literal method unless the text itself mentions a figurative or symbolic interpretation.
3. The underlying purpose of God in the world is His glory

One can be a Dispensationalist and hold differing views concerning the number of dispensations, but the following tenets are believed by all Dispensationalists.

D DISPENSATIONS

DISPENSATIONS

Divisions of time in which mankind responds to a specific revelation of the will of God. I believe in a literal, dispensational interpretation of God's Word "rightly dividing" it (2 Timothy 2:15). There are seven dispensations:

1. Innocence — Creation to the fall (Genesis 1:27; 3:24)
2. Conscience — Beginning of civilization to the Flood (Genesis 4:1; 8:14)
3. Human Government — Exit from the Ark to the Tower of Babel (Genesis 8:15; 11:32)
4. Promise — Call of Abraham to Egyptian bondage (Genesis 12:1; Exodus 19:2)
5. Law — Ten Commandments to the end of the Gospels (Exodus 19:3; Acts 1)
6. Grace — Pentecost to end of the Tribulation (Acts 2; Revelation 19:21)
7. Millennium (Kingdom) — Imprisonment of Satan to the Great White Throne (Revelation 20:1; 22:7)

DISTRESS OF NATIONS (See Signs)

DRAGON

Another name for Satan (Revelation 12).

DRUG ABUSE (See Signs)

EARTHQUAKES (See Signs)

ELDERS, TWENTY-FOUR

John foresaw this group of men around the throne of God. It is my opinion that the 24 elders represent God's people in both testaments — 12 tribal patriarchs and 12 apostles — the saints of both testaments. The Book of Revelation unites them often. In describing the Holy City in Revelation 21:12-14, the names of the 12 tribes of Israel are posted on the gates while the names of the 12 apostles are inscribed upon the city's foundations.

We witness the saints of all ages in Revelation 4:10,11, praising the Lamb of God for shedding His blood and casting their crowns down before Him.

There are two alternative views as to the identity of the 24 elders. One holds that they are angelic beings while another view insists they are New Testament saints only. Dr. Pentecost holds the latter view as does Rev. Rouse, with some support.

ELECT, THE

God has two elect groups of individuals on this earth, Israel and the Church. There is no difficulty whatsoever when men see both elections, but confusion reigns when the two are intermingled. Israel was chosen (elected) by Jehovah to be His wife forever (Deuteronomy 7:6) and the Church was chosen (elected) by Christ to be His Bride (John 15:16; Ephesians 1:4).

Because of their history of rejection of Jesus Christ as Messiah (Saviour), God, in His foreknowledge, has set up a different schedule for the Jews as a nation than for the Church all the way through history until the Millennium, or Kingdom Age. Because the true Church, all born-again believers, wholeheartedly accepts Christ as Saviour (John 1:11,12), they are called to heaven escaping the Tribulation period, or Time of Jacob's Trouble (see Rapture). During this time of disillusionment over their false messiah (the Antichrist) and their horrifying persecution at his hand, the Jews as a nation

47

will finally recognize Jesus Christ as Messiah and King in the midst of their suffering (Romans 11). This clarifies Matthew 24:22 which states, *But for the elect's sake* [Israel, Deuteronomy 7:6] *those days shall be shortened.*

The Judgment Seat of Christ for the Church occurs in the heavenlies as the Tribulation judgment hits the earth. Both "elect" groups are being prepared for the Millennium. At the conclusion of this Time of Jacob's Trouble, Christ returns with an army of believers and judges the nations on the basis of their rejection of Christ and their treatment of Israel (Matthew 25:31-46).

ELIJAH

Malachi records that Elijah will return before the coming of the great and dreadful Day of the Lord and his coming will accomplish the repentance and conversion of God's people, Israel (Malachi 3:1; 4:5,6; Matthew 11:14; Luke 1:17). Some interpreters say this prophecy was fulfilled completely in John the Baptist. Others feel the prophecy was only partially fulfilled in John the Baptist and has a still future aspect during the Tribulation. Some of these believe that Elijah will be one of the two witnesses (see Witnesses, Two), while others believe another will come *in the spirit and power of Elijah* (Luke 1:17) as John the Baptist did.

Most Bible scholars believe that the witnesses are either Elijah and Moses or Elijah and Enoch. There is no doubt about Elijah being one of the witnesses. Malachi's prediction is corroborated by the fact that Elijah did not die a physical death but was taken up into heaven by a whirlwind and chariot of fire (2 Kings 2:9-11) (see Witnesses, Two).

EPIPHANEIA (See Christ, Coming of)

ESCHATOLOGY

Eschatology is the study of "last things" or prophecy.

It has been observed that approximately 25 percent of the Bible deals with prophetic truth. That means that at

EUPHRATES RIVER **E**

the time of its writing, one-fourth of scripture was pre-written history. Many prophecies have come to pass, but much of God's Word is yet to be fulfilled (Dr. Bob Shelton).

Biblical Eschatology is the capstone of systematic theology. More than any other major field of theology, it has suffered much at the hands of its interpreters. Even among those whose confidence in the inspired Word of God is unquestioned there exists widely divergent schools of interpretation (Dr. J. D. Pentecost).

ETERNAL LIFE

The gift of God to every believer in Christ at his salvation (Ephesians 2:8; John 3:16; 17:3). It is not merely endless life which all men possess, but life united with God for all eternity. Everlasting separation from God is eternal death while everlasting union with God is eternal life. The natural, unconverted man will spend eternity in the Lake of Fire (Revelation 21:8).

ETERNITY

Time which has no beginning and no ending. It is an attribute of God (Isaiah 57:15; Psalm 90:2). When all the ages are totaled, they add up to eternity (2 Timothy 4:18).

EUPHRATES RIVER

There is a striking similarity between the sixth trumpet judgment (Revelation 9:13-18) and the sixth tipped bowl (Revelation 16:12). The sixth angel voices his commands and four fallen angels are loosed from the great river Euphrates, the area of present-day Iran and Iraq. A total of 200 million troops appear in the Middle East from the Orient. The Euphrates dries up in order that the kings of the East might cross over to fight the Battle of Armageddon.

Both chapters 9 and 16 mention the Euphrates River as a focal point in this war. The Euphrates belonged to Iran and Iraq when both nations were called Persia.

There will be a fiery holocaust and one-third of mankind will die (Revelation 9:18).

EZEKIEL'S PROPHECY

In the last days, the Russian people will look with covetous eyes upon the great developments in the land of Israel. They will want the wealth produced there. Consequently, a vast army, augmented by warriors from Persia, Cush, and Phut, march toward Israel (Ezekiel 38-39; see Russia).

FALLEN ANGELS (See Angels)

FALSE ACCUSERS (See Signs)

FALSE CHRISTS (See Signs)

FALSE PROPHET

He is the religious leader who ascends to world popularity via his close alignment with the Antichrist. He is a religious fake (Revelation 13:11), yet he is the leader of the one-world church described in Revelation 17. His main role is honoring the Antichrist (Revelation 13:12). He will work unbelievable miracles (Revelation 13:13), lead people into idolatry (worshipping the Image of the Beast, the Antichrist), and execute people in the name of religion. He will be tormented with the Antichrist in the Lake of Fire (Revelation 19:20; 20:10) after the Lord Jesus Christ returns to earth to fight the armies gathered together for Armageddon.

FAMINE (See Signs)

FIERCE (uncontrolled temper) (See Signs)

FIG TREE

Joel pictures Israel as the fig tree (Joel 1:7)(Hosea 9:10). Israel's existence today is the fulfillment of the reference in Matthew 24:32 to the blossoming of the fig tree.

FIGURATIVE LANGUAGE (See Interpretation, Methods)

FIRE (See Days of Lot; Nuclear War)

FOREHEAD

In the endtime, the forehead will be used for identification purposes. Millions enslaved by the Antichrist will receive a mark in their foreheads containing the name of the Beast and his number which is 666 (Revelation 13:16-18). The woman of Revelation 17, representing the false church, will carry the name, *Mystery, Babylon the Great, the Mother of Harlots, and Abominations of the Earth* on her forehead. On the other side, we see that believers remaining faithful will receive the name of God, the New Jerusalem, and Jesus' new name written upon them (Revelation 3:12), and the 144,000 Jewish evangelists will also receive a seal upon their foreheads (Revelation 7:3).

FORNICATION

This word is especially descriptive of the unfaithful works of the false church, the professing, but not possessing, Bride of Christ. This "spiritual fornication" committed between worldly leaders and the Church actually began with Constantine in the year 312. It has continued through the centuries, but under the leadership of the False Prophet, the world church will be at its worst as it practices idolatry, worshipping the image of the world leader, the Antichrist. Of course, the true Church will be raptured by the time this occurs (Revelation 17:1,2; 14:8).

FOUR HORSEMAN (See Horses)

FULLNESS OF TIMES

That period of time which brings about the "consummation of God's plan through Messiah" (Ephesians 1:10).

There are three interpretations of this phrase:
1. Non-premillennialist view — the term speaks of the gospel of this present age
2. Pre-millennialist view — the term speaks of the Millennium
3. Also pre-millennialist view — the term speaks of the eternal state (see Millennium, Views of).

GEHENNA

This term, used 12 times in the New Testament, literally means "Valley of Hinnom" that became a natural symbol of hell. It was a place where King Ahaz introduced the sacrifice of little children to the god Moloch (1 Kings 11:7). This place became so detested that it was used as a dump for all kinds of refuse that burned continually. It is equivalent to the Lake of Fire. As Hades can be considered a jail or holding place (see Hades), Gehenna, or the Lake of Fire, is like the final penitentiary where there will be degrees of punishment (Romans 2:5). In the following scriptures, Christ refers to Gehenna, translated hell or hell fire: Matthew 5:22,29,30; 10:28; 18:9; 23:15; 23:33; Mark 9:43-47. Revelation 20:13,14 pictures the moment Gehenna becomes operative for the judged.

GENERATION

Although no one can know the day and hour of Christ's return (Matthew 24:36), we can know the generation (vs. 34). When all the signs occur simultaneously, it is at the door (Matthew 24:33). It is felt that a generation is approximately 51.5 years.

GENTILES, FULLNESS OF

This term depicts a time when the fulfilled number of Gentiles will be saved (Romans 11:25). When God completes His purpose, taking out of the Gentiles a *people for his name* (Acts 15:14), and the full number of these are saved, Christ will return for His own at the Rapture. Immediately following, the Tribulation will take place and multitudes of Gentiles from all nations, kindreds, and people turn to Christ as a result of the preaching of the 144,000 Jewish evangelists who reach every corner of the world (Revelation 7:14). These Gentiles, however, are not part of the Church or Bride, but that of a new dispensation. There is no possibility that the nation of Israel will turn to the Lord before the fullness of the Gentiles comes in (Romans 11:25). When the Lord returns all Israel will be saved.

GENTILES, TIMES OF THE

This is the period of time during which Jerusalem has been or is under the domination of Gentiles . . . beginning with the Babylonian captivity and ending with Armageddon at the conclusion of the Tribulation Hour. Control of the city of Jerusalem may shift back and forth, but once Armageddon is finished, it will be controlled by the Jews forevermore (Luke 21:20-24). The fact that Jews have been in control of Jerusalem since the Six Day War of 1967 is exciting as this has not happened for 2,500 years.

GOG AND MAGOG (See Russia)

GOSPEL OF THE KINGDOM (See Signs)

The "gospel of the kingdom" is the message that the King is coming. The King came, was rejected temporarily (John 1:11), and the Dispensation of Grace began. It continues until the Rapture. Then, during the Tribulation period, 144,000 again proclaim the gospel of the kingdom. If one wonders how one is saved during kingdom times, read on as it duplicates John's message. John's message was repentance (Matthew 3:2) and the blood (John 1:29), for he said, *Behold the Lamb of God, which taketh away the sin of the world.* How? . . . Hear John again . . . By Christ who loved us and washed us from our sins in His own blood (Revelation 1:5). John warned the people that the King was coming, preaching repentance and the sacrifice of Christ. The 144,000 will preach the same message.

GREAT WHITE THRONE JUDGMENT

This judgment includes all the wicked of all time, resurrected for this hour (John 5:28,29; Acts 24:15; 1 Corinthians 16:22,24). The Lord Jesus Christ sits on a throne (Romans 2:16; John 6:27; Acts 17:31) and the books (records) are opened. The list of sins judged are found in Revelation 21:8; 22:15; Romans 1:24-32; 1 Corinthians 6:9,10; and Galatians 5:19-21, plus many others named throughout Scripture (see Sin).

At the final judgment, it is forever too late to repent. Judgment for breaking God's laws must now be administered according to the individual's wicked works (Revelation 20:12). However, I insert this word of hope.

Now is the day of salvation (2 Corinthians 6:2). God loves sinners and will save all who seek His remedy — salvation through Jesus. *For God sent not his Son into the world to condemn the world, but that the world through him might be saved* (John 3:17). That's why God, after listing ten of the vilest of sins in 1 Corinthians 6:9,10, adds this word of comfort in verse 11, *And such were some of you: But you are washed.* How can you be washed from every sin that would bring you into judgment? The Holy Spirit answers that question in Revelation 1:5 by saying, *Unto Christ, who loved us and washed us from our sins in His own blood . . . .*

So you have a choice. Judge your own sin now, confess your sin to God, and ask Christ to cleanse and save you. When this is done, Judgment Day is canceled because, *There is therefore now no condemnation* [judgment] *to them which are in Christ Jesus* (Romans 8:1). However, *he that believeth not is judged* (John 3:18).

HEALING OF NATIONS **H**

HADES

Hades was the place where the souls and the spirits of all humans went until the cross. Sheol (Old Testament) and Hades (New Testament) are one and the same. In Sheol or Hades there were two compartments, one for the wicked and the other for the righteous . . . one for suffering and the other for comfort (Luke 16:22,23). The thief on the cross went to the comfort side, or Paradise, as promised by Christ (Luke 23:43) (see Abraham's Bosom). This is where Christ went upon His death (Acts 2:27,31). There He ministered to His people and led captivity captive (Ephesians 4:8-10), releasing and transporting them into the third heaven of 2 Corinthians 12:2. That is why Paradise is referred to as "up" (Revelation 2:7; 2 Corinthians 12:4). So presently, the comfort side of Hades (Paradise) has been emptied by Him who has the keys of death and Hades (Revelation 20:13).

Of course, the suffering side of Hades still teems with the wicked as the unregenerate continue to die day by day and are added to its population. They have joined the rich man of Luke 16:23 and will not come out again until Judgment Day when they will meet Christ at their trial and be transferred to the final penitentiary of lost souls, Gehenna (Revelation 20:13,14). Christ describes Hades 11 times in the New Testament: Matthew 11:23; 16:18; Luke 10:15; 16:22,23; Acts 2:27,31; Revelation 1:18; 6:8; 20:13,14.

HARLOT, GREAT (See Babylon, Mystery)

HEALING OF NATIONS

This term, found in Revelation 22:2, should read "health of the nations." The tree of life in the Holy City contains health for the nations living under, or in the light of, that city hovering above the earth. Since there is no sorrow, sickness, or pain, healing is unnecessary. Health is in forever.

HEARTS FAILING (See Signs)

HEAVENS, FIRST, SECOND, AND THIRD

Jesus spoke about two places in eternity, heaven and hell (Matthew 7:13,14,21; 25:41,46; Luke 16:22-24) (see Hell). Death is not a sad ending but a glorious beginning (John 14:1-6). Heaven is so real that God gives details concerning its location. His Word speaks of three heavens:

The third heaven is God's holy hemisphere (2 Corinthians 12:2,3).

It is upward and in the north. Elijah was caught *up* by a whirlwind into heaven (2 Kings 2:11; Psalm 48:2; 75:6; Isaiah 14:13; Acts 1:9).

Astronomers tell us there is an opening in the universe to get to this third heaven. It is in the north, in the constellation of "Swan." Job 26:7 says, *He stretcheth out the north over the empty place*. To understand the word, "paradise," see Hades, or Abraham's Bosom.

HEAVENS AND EARTH, NEW AND OLD

The present earth and heaven will be completely renovated after the Great White Throne Judgement by something similar to a nuclear blast (2 Peter 3:10,11). One of the heavens referred to here is at least the first heaven, the atmosphere which has been defiled because of Satan and his wickedness (Ephesians 2:2). It's also possible that the destruction of the second heaven from whence Satan makes His accusations against the brethren to God (who dwells in the third heaven, Revelation 12:10), happens at this point of time. The reason for this is to refine the old world (Isaiah 65:17). God will then present us with a new heaven and a new earth (Revelation 21:1,2,10).

HELL (See Lake of Fire)

Two Greek words translated "hell" in the New

Testament are *Hades* and *Gehenna*. The temporary holding place or "local jail" is Hades, while Gehenna refers to the final penitentiary for lost souls. The Lake of Fire is usually synonymous with Gehenna. Gehenna differs from Hades also in that Gehenna is a place where there are degrees of suffering. Thus, the final hell will differ for all depending on one's evil deeds and the number of times he rejected Christ (Romans 2:5; Matthew 11:23,24; 23:14) (see Hades, Gehenna). Order my full-length cassette on this subject.

HINDERER (See Holy Spirit)

HISTORICAL INTERPRETATION (See Interpretation, Methods of)

HOLOCAUSTS

The first holocaust was carried out in 70 A.D. when Titus and his army entered Jerusalem, cut down all the trees, and carried out hundreds of executions. Josephus, the historian, says that 1,100,000 Jews were slain and thousands taken into captivity. The Temple was burned and even the stones were pried apart to retrieve precious metals that had melted between them.

Hitler's holocaust reduced the population of European Jews from 9,739,200 in 1939 to 3,505,130. His death camps and portable killing units had exterminated six million of the Children of Israel by 1945.

In the future, midway through the Tribulation period, the alleged peacemaker, Antichrist, will break his covenant or treaty with the Jews and will become their enemy and persecutor. Anti-Semitism will flourish and Israel will experience her final holocaust. It is called the Time of Jacob's Trouble (Jeremiah 30:7). This will be the worst time in history (Matthew 24:21). It is also called Daniel's Seventieth Week, the Great Tribulation. At this moment in history, the whole world will plunge into its most awful hour and the Jews will be the universal scapegoat (Matthew 24:15-22).

HOLY CITY

This beautiful city, prepared by Christ for His beloved, and promised to John over 1,900 years ago, is also called the New Jerusalem. It's foundations, walls, and gates are described in detail in Revelation 21 and 22 along with its measurements and other lovely attractions. There are mansions there, but no temple because the Lord God has chosen to dwell with men and needs no other dwelling place (Revelation 21:3,22). The Lamb (Christ) is the very light of it. When that light shines through the brilliancy of the layers of precious stones, all will surely know the "glory of God." Two other important attractions are the tree of life (last seen in the Garden of Eden) and the river of "the pure water of life" proceeding out of the throne of God.

This city, built foursquare, will hover in space and the people on the new earth will live in the light of it (Revelation 21:24). Those living in the Holy City will be able to travel back and forth between the two places effortlessly and miraculously (see Bodies, Glorified and Natural). Men are now designing space cities, but none like this!

It is from this heavenly city that David's greater son (Jesus) exerts His messianic rule, in which the Bride reigns, and from which the rewarded Old Testament saints exercise their authority in government. (Dr. J. D. Pentecost)

HOLY SPIRIT

This person of the Holy Trinity, also called "the Comforter" by Jesus Christ (John 16:7,8), came to dwell in believers when Jesus returned to heaven. It is evident that the work of the Holy Spirit is that of conviction and restraint concerning sin in those whose bodies He indwells (1 Corinthians 6:19).

He always glorifies Christ. Believers have a purifying effect upon the world (Matthew 5:13,14). No wonder the world is so wicked during the Tribulation — the believers are gone in the Rapture and the restraining influence of the Holy Spirit with them (2 Thessalonians 2:1-8). This must not be interpreted to mean that the Holy Spirit is no longer omnipresent, nor operative during the Tribulation Hour. At this time He will work in and through men as He did in Old Testament times. His particular ministries to the believer in this present age are: baptism into the body of Christ (1 Corinthians 12:12,13), indwelling (1 Corinthians 6:19,20), sealing (Ephesians 1:13, 4:30), and filling (Ephesians 5:18). During the Tribulation period He will return to working as He did in Old Testament times and will anoint the 144,000 Jewish evangelists for service (Revelation 7:2,3; Joel 2:28,29).

He is the restrainer (2 Timothy 2: 7,8).

1. As the wicked one is a personality with operations in the spiritual realm, so is the Holy Spirit and therefore able to hold Antichrist in check until the time for his revealing.

2. The restrainer must be a member of the Godhead, stronger than the man of sin and Satan who energizes him. In order to restrain evil down through the ages, He must be eternal.

3. The Church Age began with the Spirit's baptism at Pentecost and will close with a reversal of Pentecost . . . the removal of the indwelling Spirit by the Rapture (catching away) of those He indwells, the believers. This does not mean that He will not be operative on earth during the Tribulation . . . only that He will no longer be resident in believers.

HORNS

Horns denote national powers (Revelation 13:1). The "little horn" is also another name for Antichrist (Daniel 7:8; 8:9). The little horn arises out of the fourth beast which represents Rome; so it is supposed that the Antichrist will rise out of the revived Roman Empire. This term is also used of Antiochus Epiphanes (Daniel 8-9) (see Ten Nation Conspiracy . . . 10 horns).

H HORSES

HORSES

The four horsemen of Revelation 6 are:

1. The white horse whose rider is Antichrist (vs. 29), counterfeits the return of Christ and produces a fraudulent peace pact (Revelation 19:11).

2. The red horse (vs. 4) produces wars and rumors of wars. Perhaps Russia (red) might have a part here.

3. The black horse (vs. 8), produces famine and inflation as the 666 program becomes activated.

4. The pale horse (vs. 8), the deadliest, produces death and disease with hell following him.

Countless horses will be utilized by the armies of Armageddon as the blood rises to their bridles (Revelation 14:20), and Christ himself will return, mounted on a white horse, followed by His armies also riding white horses (Revelation 19:11-14).

IMAGE, NEBUCHADNEZZAR'S (See
Nebuchadnezzar's Dream)

IMAGE OF THE BEAST
The False Prophet will entice mankind to build the greatest statue in history, the image of the Antichrist. This monstrosity will be placed in the Jewish temple. Since the image speaks and is built by mankind, it may well be the ultimate achievement of our present-day computer systems. There is, at present, a master computer in Luxembourg that can handle facts and figures on everyone in the world. Antichrist will most certainly use it, or a similar computer.

There is the likelihood that the number six was the base of civilization's first system of computation (Zondervan Pictorial Encyclopedia of the Bible, Vol. 4). Add to this the fact that every language of the world had a common source. A gematria has been formed by adding the number "6" to each letter of the alphabet (A=6, B=12, C=18, etc.). Using this system, words can be computed. On the instruction of Revelation 13:18, it is interesting to note that mark+of+beast equals 666 as does computer . . . interesting! (Rev. Jerry R. Church, founder and director of *Prophecy in the News*, Oklahoma City, Oklahoma)

Nineteen hundred years ago, when God told the Apostle John that the endtimes would produce an image that spoke, it was beyond his comprehension, but today we witness its beginning. Professor Seymour Wolfson has featured a talking robot, in a science seminar, whose brain capacity equaled that of one trillion human beings.

I IMMINENCY

IMMORTALITY

Immortality means everlasting. A quality of life which God enjoys by nature (1 Timothy 6:16). Believers, in their glorified bodies, will also be free from any deterioration that the power of death works (1 Corinthians 15:53,54).

INCONTINENT (See Signs)

INIQUITY (See Signs)

INTERPRETATION, METHODS OF

No question facing the student of prophecy is more important than which method he will use in interpreting the prophetic scriptures. Differing methods explain divergent views such as premillennial schools, amillennial schools, or postmillennial schools (the latter being revived under the label, Dominion Theology), pretribulation and posttribulation rapturists, etc. The system adopted determines the meaning of the Word of God so it is extremely important that a correct method and sound rules for interpretation be used. The question to be answered is, "What, exactly, does a text mean and to whom is it addressed?"

The interpreter must give each passage only one interpretation although applications may be many. Application, or exposition, is the deduction of spiritual truths, principles, and concepts from that which has been literally interpreted. Therefore, it must be in line with one interpretation.

Double Reference Interpretation:

Many prophecies contain both a near and far view. This is illustrated by the use of a telescope. Much will be added to what is seen with the naked eye when the telescope is used. Certain scriptures, when viewed by the original readers, will have a particular application, but when viewed in the light of further revelation, another, further application will be seen. The prophet had a message for his own day as well as for a future time. Only God could bring the two widely separated events into the scope of the prophecy and see both purposes fulfilled.

Figurative Method of Interpretation:

The literal statements of Scripture are allegedly taken to stand for a higher, spiritual meaning. This is also called the allegorical method and sets aside the literal and historical sense, especially in the area of prophecy. This, of course, is restricted only by the imagination of the interpreter, allowing for a great deal of latitude.

Literal Method of Interpretation:

Each word is taken in its literal, normal sense. This method allows for symbols and figures of speech when the context clearly requires them and the language is understood as it is normally used. It has been said, "If common sense makes good sense, seek no other sense." Each word ought to be taken at its simplest, literal meaning unless the context or related passages of Scripture make clear that it is to be otherwise understood.

Of course, this is not always easy. For example, in prophecy, we find locusts that look like "horses prepared unto battle," wearing crowns like gold, with faces like men, hair as that of women, teeth like that of lions, wearing "as it were" breastplates of iron (Revelation 9:1-11)! Although we have never observed such creatures, they certainly will appear in the Tribulation! Cloning might make it happen soon. Recent science releases on genetic tampering with animals indicate that such monstrosities could be created. Whenever the word "like" or "as" is used, great care should be taken not to become ridiculous, but rational.

I INTERPRETATION, METHODS OF

ISRAEL

It is impossible to grasp God's prophetic plan apart from an understanding of His promises to Israel.

The Jews have enriched all nations in which they have settled because of God's promise to Abraham (Genesis 12:2), yet no people have suffered so consistently as have the descendants of Abraham, Isaac, and Jacob. Mark Twain once wrote, "Jews constitute but one percent of the human race. His commercial importance is extravagantly out of proportion to the smallness of his bulk. His contributions to the world's list of great names in every field is also out of proportion to the weakness of his numbers . . . and he has done it with his hands tied behind him" (see Deuteronomy 28:37). Although he is such a contributor, the Jew himself is unwanted, often persecuted. Why this "blessing and cursing"? (see Deuteronomy 28:65-67, 30:19,20). God has always kept His promises to His people (blessing), but has always warned what would happen to them if they turned away from following after Him (Deuteronomy 28:45-48).

God promised Abraham in Genesis 12:2,3, that He would make of him a great nation. He would bless those who blessed his descendants, curse those who cursed them, and all the world would be blessed because of them. He also promised them all the land of Canaan as an everlasting possession (Genesis 17:8). The boundaries of this promised land are found in Genesis 15:18-21.

Since Daniel's interpretation of King Nebuchadnezzar's dream, the Jews have been awaiting a Messiah (Saviour) to deliver them and set up His kingdom on earth, reigning from Jerusalem (Daniel 2:44). Daniel 9:24 pointed out when He would come and that He

would be rejected by the Jews. This is exactly what happened. Precisely 483 years to the day, after the issuing of the decree to build Jerusalem, the Messiah came riding into Jerusalem as had been prophesied (Zechariah 9:9). (The final 7 years totaling and fulfilling 490, account for the time of the Tribulation, Daniel's Seventieth Week.)

Messiah, the Prince, Jesus Christ was rejected by His people. He was cut off (crucified), but not for himself; He died for others. At that moment, the prophetic clock stopped as far as Daniel's vision is concerned and 70 years later the Jews were dispossessed of their country and scattered throughout the world.

Following their rejection of Messiah, the Jews entered upon their longest period of suffering and persecution. For centuries, Jewish blood has been spilled across Europe and other parts of the world from the destruction of Jerusalem in 70 A.D. on through Hitler's ovens in 1945. The Jewish ability to remain a people apart while scattered throughout the world is another evidence of the divine plan.

Through the death of Christ, the wall between Jews and Gentiles was broken down and they now become brothers, or one in Christ at the moment of new birth (Ephesians 2:13-15). Jews can be reconciled to God on an individual basis just as Gentiles can (Colossians 1:20-22).

The same Word of God that announced their dispersion guarantees their return to the land God promised them (Jeremiah 31:10,11) and Ezekiel's vision of the dry bones in chapter 37 was prophetic of what happened in 1948 when Israel finally became a nation. This began the prophecy of the desert blossoming "as a rose" (Isaiah 35:1) and the budding of the fig tree in Matthew 24:32-34, heralding the "generation" that would live to see "all things fulfilled."

However, the Jews cannot rest yet, they must be ever vigilant as there is much hostility around them. One day they will sign a peace treaty with many nations. It will be an agreement intended to last for seven years

(Daniel 9:27). At that point the Tribulation period will begin (see Daniel's Seventieth Week; Jacob's Trouble, Time of; Tribulation).

Daniel's vision and seventieth week will resume for the Tribulation. It must be remembered that the Tribulation is especially related to Israel. Once this truth is established, all confusion about the time of the Rapture disappears. The return of Christ for His Church marks the end of the Church Age, the parenthetical period, and begins the Time of Jacob's Trouble (see Tribulation, Jacob's Trouble). Shortly after the Rapture, there will be a remnant of Jews who turn to Christ. The initial number is 144,000, 12,000 from each of the 12 tribes of Israel (Revelation 7:4-8). They will evangelize the world and a great multitude from all nations will be converted to Christ proving their faith by martyrdom.

Many Jews who do not turn to Christ during the Tribulation Hour will return to temple worship as in Old Testament times, including the sacrifice of animals (Ezekiel 40-48). It may well be that the erection of the Temple in Jerusalem will be a part of the peace agreement between the final world dictator and the Jews. Ultimately, however, Antichrist will take control of Jewish worship, declaring himself to be God and demanding worship from the Jews in their own Temple (2 Thessalonians 2:4) (see Abomination of Desolation, Matthew 24:15). After their betrayal by Antichrist, midway through the Tribulation period (Daniel 9:27), Israel will experience her final holocaust.

Russia will invade Israel at a time when war is not expected (Ezekiel 38-39) (see Russia). It appears this invasion will come about the middle of the Tribulation period (approximately three and one-half years after signing the peace treaty.

It seems that Antichrist will come to world power at that point in time as the extension of his dominion over all the earth seems to follow the defeat of Russia and the armies of the East (Revelation 9:16). However, the contrasting reality of divine protection of Israel will turn many Jews to their Messiah, the Lord Jesus Christ, and great numbers will be called upon to seal their testimonies with blood.

Furious over the success of the 144,000 evangelists and bitter because many Jews have rejected his rule having turned to Jesus Christ, this dictator will announce a campaign to destroy the Jewish race once and for all. He will blame them for every ill on earth and summon the armies of the earth to the Middle East to destroy them and defeat their Messiah at His coming. Armageddon will end the rebellion of man as the enemies of the Lord are defeated (Revelation 19:11-21). Christ will finally bring peace to Israel and the world as the Saviour of men sets up His long awaited kingdom on earth. The Jews will dwell in peace in Israel, the land of their fathers (Ezekiel 36:28; Daniel 2:44) (see Millennium).

ISRAEL, CONVERSION OF

The national repentance and regeneration of Israel will finally take place at the close of the Tribulation (Jeremiah 31:33,34; Ezekiel 11:19; Zechariah 12:9-13; 113:9; Romans 11:26,27). This conversion prepares them to enter into the promised blessings of the millennial kingdom.

ISRAEL, DISPERSION OF (Diaspora)

The colonization of the Jews around the world, both voluntarily (1 Kings 20:34) and especially through deportation by conquering armies (Deuteronomy 28:64-67; 2 Kings 15:29; 17:6; Ezekiel 22:15; 36:19; John 7:35; James 1:1).

By New Testament times, it is estimated that more Jews lived outside of Palestine than in its borders. Note the number of countries represented at Pentecost as Jews returned for their festivities (Acts 2:9-11).

ISRAEL, REGATHERING

The miraculous return of Israel to her promised land

I ISRAEL, REGATHERING

after years of exile (Deuteronomy 30:3,4; Isaiah 11:11,12; Amos 9:14,15). This prophecy began to be fulfilled with the Zionist movement in 1897. The rebirth of the nation in 1948 was certainly at least a partial fulfillment of this prophecy, but if the Lord should tarry His return, there will be time for many more Jews to return. When the Messiah appears, the prophecy will be fulfilled in its entirety (Romans 11:26).

Persecution has quite often been the means God has used to encourage the Jews to return.

JACOB'S TROUBLE

Jacob *is* Israel (Jeremiah 30:7; Romans 11:26). This period of time is also called "Daniel's Seventieth Week" (Daniel 9). In history, the first 69 weeks involve Israel (9:24) and it follows that the seventieth or final week must also involve Israel. Chapters 30 and 31 of Jeremiah summarize Israel's endurance in the hour of Tribulation. All Old Testament prophets affirm this truth. In Ezekiel 38,39, seventeen different passages mark Israel as the victim of Gog and Magog's deadliest war.

Jacob's trouble is so named because of Jeremiah's prophecy: *Alas! for that day is great so that none is like it; it is even the Time of Jacob's Trouble* (Jeremiah 30:7). He was speaking of the seven-year period known as the Tribulation. With the removal of the Church (see Church Age), earth plunges into its most horrendous hour (Matthew 24:21) (see Daniel's Seventieth Week; Tribulation).

JERUSALEM

Although its history is one of war and destruction, Jerusalem means "city of peace" or "foundation of peace."

From the siege of David in 1000 B.C. to the Six Day War of 1967, the sounds of battle have been heard as this city has experienced 46 sieges and 32 partial destructions. It has been burned to the ground five times, always rising from the ashes. In the past 25 years, it has been the scene of four wars. It is the site of the most volatile political, religious, and military problems in the entire world.

The Jewish cry for peace in Jerusalem is sincere, finding its roots in the promise given through Moses (Leviticus 26:6). Jerusalem will finally become the city of peace and capital of the world when Christ, who is our peace, returns (Isaiah 9:6).

Having a history of 4,000 years, Jerusalem was first mentioned in Scripture in Genesis 14:18 when Melchizedek was king over the city of Salem. Later, it was called Jebus, named for the third son of Canaan, as it was the dwelling place of the Jebusites (Judges 19:10,11; 1 Chronicles 11:4,5).

When David took the city, the fortress was on a hill called Zion, another name given Jerusalem. Somehow, later, Jeru was added to Salem . . . perhaps a combination of Jebus, changed to Jeru, and Salem.

Since B.C. 400, Jerusalem has passed from one Gentile power to another. From 70 A.D. alone, the transition of power went from the Roman conquerors to the Persians in 614; to Caliph Omar in 637; to the Crusaders in 1099; to Salidan in 1187; to the Egyptian Mamalukes in 1250; the Turks in 1517; the British in 1917, and finally, in 1967, the Jews captured Jerusalem.

In Luke 21:24-28, Jesus said the Jews would be scattered throughout the world and the city of Jerusalem would be controlled by Gentile powers until the time of His return. In 1967, after the Six Day War was won, the Jews took control of Jerusalem for the first time in over 2,000 years.

A peace settlement in the Middle East is one of the most important events predicted for the endtime. The signing of this treaty will start the final countdown of 2,520 days leading to Armageddon. The key issue in negotiations will be the city of Jerusalem itself, which Israel prizes more than any other possession (Psalm 137:5,6). Undoubtedly a strong attempt will be made to make Jerusalem an international city with free access for Jews, Christians, and Muslims (the Temple area will also be internationalized). Jerusalem will keep center stage as this Temple becomes the scene of the Abomination of Desolation, the ultimate in desecration as the Image of the Beast is used to carry forth a diabolical plot from this holy place (Revelation 13:13-18).

Jerusalem is where the Lord touches down at His Second Coming to earth (Zechariah 14:4) and where He establishes His headquarters (Micah 4:1; Isaiah 2:3). The gates of Jerusalem will open to welcome the coming King (Psalm 24). During the Millennium, multitudes will come from the uttermost parts of the earth to visit the Holy City (Isaiah 2:2,3).

JERUSALEM, NEW

Two Jerusalems are mentioned in Scripture (Galatians 4:25,26; Hebrews 12:22). One is the earthly home of the believers during the millennial period. The other is heavenly — the New Jerusalem, or celestial city, which hovers over the earth eternally.

Christ has been preparing this new Jerusalem for 2,000 years (John 14:2). This magnificent masterpiece descending toward earth reminds one of the elegant beauty of a bride on her wedding day (Revelation 21:2). Verses 9-27 present a glowing description of the city.

The Almighty will handle global operations from this satellite city. The redeemed in glorified bodies will live there and travel back and forth to earth from their city in space in a moment of time. Resurrection and rapture are the only ways to obtain glorified bodies. Those with bodies of flesh, who were born during the Millennium, enter the eternal state with natural bodies and live on earth in and under the light of the Holy City (ch. 21:24).

JESUS CHRIST, LORD

In eternity past, Jesus Christ was pre-existent as part of the holy Trinity (Psalm 90:2) and He was there at the creation of the world, taking an active part (John 1:1-4; Colossians 1:16; Hebrews 1:1-3; Revelation 4:10,11).

Jesus Christ appears in prophecy as early as Genesis 3:15 and continues on through the Old Testament accounts in types and angelic appearances until He comes in the flesh as recorded in the New Testament (born to the virgin, Mary, in Bethlehem, Luke 12; Matthew 1).

The Book of Revelation concerns the unveiling or appearing of our Saviour, the Lord Jesus Christ (Revelation 1:1). This appearing takes place at the Rapture (4:1), as well as at the hour of His return to earth when every eye shall see Him (1:7; 19:11) (see Rapture; Revelation). He is referred to symbolically as the Lion of Judah, the Lamb of God, the Alpha and Omega, and the Light of the World, among many other names descriptive of His personage and mission. Five times He is called "the only begotten" Son of God, referring to His incarnation. Yet, He has no beginning as He is from old, from everlasting and as part of the Trinity, one with the everlasting Father (Micah 5:2; Isaiah 9:6).

He is also called "first begotten" or "firstborn" five times, referring to His resurrection, even though others such as Lazarus, were raised first. Others, raised from death to physical life, eventually died a second time. Christ was raised from the dead to immortality (Acts 26:23; 1 Timothy 6:16; Romans 8:29 . . . never to die again . . . hence the first begotten.

Christ's three-fold work on our behalf is described in Revelation 1:5,6.

1. He loves us forever (John 13:1; Romans 8:37-39)

2. He washed us from our sins in His own precious blood (Titus 3:5)

3. He made us kings and priests unto God His Father (Revelation 1:6)

He fulfilled prophecy at His coming (see Christ, Prophecies Fulfilled). His life is a matter of historical record and His Second Coming is described in detail in both testaments.

He uses the title, "I am," which is a verb indicating being, not becoming. He said, *Before Abraham was, I AM* (John 8:58; Colossians 1:16). He controls all things (Hebrews 1:3) and He will consummate all things as well (Ephesians 1:10).

Christ's Second Coming is in two phases. The first part is when He comes *for* His own (see Rapture). The second part is when He comes *with* His own to conquer at Armageddon and to set up His kingdom where He will reign as King of Kings and Lord of Lords (Revelation 19:11-16) (see Revelation).

He is described in the first chapter of the Book of Revelation as having white hair, depicting antiquity; as having brazen feet, depicting judgment. The sight of Jesus Christ glorified is so breathtaking, that John, who laid his head upon Jesus at the Last Supper, now falls prostrate at His feet.

He is the One that liveth (resurrection), was dead (crucifixion), and who cries, *Behold, I am alive forevermore* (resurrection and ascension), Amen (vs. 18). He also holds the keys of hell and of death. Because of this, Christians need not fear. Not only has He delivered us from the fear of death, but from the fear of hell (Hebrews 2:14,15).

Because of this, He is the only One worthy to open the book (Revelation 5:5,9). Christ, as the Lamb of God (John 1:29), earned the right by redemption to open the seals on the book (the title deed to the earth) beginning the work of judgment in the Tribulation.

Christ is the lion of the tribe of Judah, the root of David. Since Judah is the leading tribe of Israel and a lion is the king of beasts, Christ is thus pictured when He comes as Israel's king (Revelation 19:16). It is at the same moment that the Lord God gives unto Him the throne of His father, David (Luke 1:32; Isaiah 9:6,7). He will reign from this throne in Jerusalem during the Millennium and the government shall be upon His shoulders.

After the Millennium, the tender, loving Jesus becomes the judge who sits upon the Great White Throne and *from whose face the earth and heaven flee away*. This is the final judgment, as unregenerate mankind comes face-to-face with a Holy God (Revelation 20:11-15).

The Lord Jesus Christ is central to the Holy City. There is no need of a temple as the Lord God Almighty and the Lamb has chosen to dwell with His people (31:3) and there is no need of the sun to shine. Jesus, *the light of the world* (John 8:12), in all His radiant splendor and glory shines forth so magnificently that darkness becomes an impossibility. No wonder there will be no night there (Revelation 21:25, 22:5).

J JEWS

JEWS

All prophetic truth revolves around the Jews. The Bible reviews their history and unfolds their future. The future of the world will be affected by the future of the Jews (see Israel).

JUDGMENT (See Signs)

JUDGMENT DAY (See Great White Throne Judgment)

JUDGMENT OF FALLEN ANGELS

This is the judgment of those angels who followed Lucifer and were cast out of heaven (Isaiah 14:12; Matthew 25:41; 2 Peter 2:4; Jude 6). Satan and these "demons" will be cast into the Lake of Fire, prepared by God for this very purpose (Matthew 25:41).

JUDGMENTS

Five different, diversified, and distinct judgments are presented in the Bible:

1. *Judgment of the believer's sin: Without the shedding of blood, there is no remission of sin* (Hebrews 9:22). Nineteen hundred years ago, Christ came down from heaven's glory to shed His precious blood for a world of ungodly sinners. He did not die for His own sin, for He knew no sin, but became sin for us (2 Corinthians 5:21). Through His substitutionary death, dying for mankind, all who receive this Christ can have the past, present, and future stains of sin forgiven and forgotten (Hebrews 8:12). The *blood of Jesus Christ,* [God's] *Son, cleanseth us from all sin* (1 John 1:7; Titus 3:5; Romans 8:1).

2. *Judgment of the believer's service:* The believer's lifetime of works are judged at the Bema Seat (2 Corinthians 5:10) (see Rapture, Bema, Judgment Seat of Christ).

3. *Judgment of Israel:* When the armies of the world converge on the Middle East, culminating at Israel (Zechariah 14:2; Ezekiel 38,39), this period of bloody

devastation becomes the Time of Jacob's Trouble (Jeremiah 30:7) (see Daniel's Seventieth Week, Jacob's Trouble).

During this Tribulation period, the whole world will come into judgment also. One in three will die by fire and one-half of all people will die during this time (Revelation 9:18). Numerous passages describe this time as the earth's worst event (Jeremiah 30:7; Daniel 12:1; Joel 2:2). Jesus said, *Then shall be great tribulation, such as was not since the beginning of the world to this time, no, nor ever shall be* (Matthew 24:21). At this time they will "look on Him whom they have pierced." Their response will cause them to repent and recognize Christ as Messiah.

4. *Judgment of the nations:* Matthew 25 pictures the return of Christ to this earth. This correlates with Revelation 19:11-16 when Christ returns as King of Kings and Lord of Lords. After Armageddon and before He establishes His millennial kingdom upon earth (Revelation 20:4), He purges the earth of its rebels. The "sheep" nations are invited to enter the kingdom (Millennium) along with the "brethren," the Jews. The "goats," those who mistreated Jews and rejected Christ, are cast into the Lake of Fire (Matthew 25:31-46; 1 Corinthians 15:24,25).

There are a total of 21 special judgments that fall upon earth during the Tribulation period. They are in three series of sevens described as seals, trumpets, and vials (or bowls):

The Seal Judgments

This is the beginning of the program of God to pour out judgments upon the earth. They include:

1. The world's greatest dictator (Revelation 6:1,2)
2. The world's greatest war (Revelation 6:3,4)
3. The world's greatest famine (Revelation 6:5,6)
4. The world's greatest death blow (Revelation 6:7,8)
5. The world's greatest persecution (Revelation 6:9,10)
6. The world's greatest ecological disaster (Revela-

tion 6:11,12)

7. The world's greatest hour of fear . . . actually the lull before the storm (Revelation 8:1)

The Trumpet Judgments

The trumpets of heaven sound an alarm throughout the world announcing the public judgments of God. Each blast ushers in an added judgment.

8. The world's greatest fire (Revelation 8:7)
9. The world's greatest oceanic disturbance (Revelation 8:8,9)
10. The world's greatest pollution of water (Revelation 8:10,11)
11. The world's greatest darkness (Revelation 8:10,11)
12. The world's greatest pestilential invasion (Revelation 9:1-6)
13. The world's greatest army (Revelation 9:16)
14. The world's greatest storm (Revelation 11:15-19)

The Vial Judgments

15. The world's greatest epidemic (Revelation 16:2)
16. The world's greatest contamination by blood (Revelation 16:3-7)
17. The world's greatest contamination by blood, continued (Revelation 16:3-7)
18. The world's greatest scorching (Revelation 16:8,9)
19. The world's greatest plague (Revelation 16:10,11)
20. The world's greatest invasion (Revelation 16:12)
21. The world's greatest earthquake (Revelation 16:18)

JUDGMENT SEAT OF CHRIST

The day is coming when every blood-bought believer must stand before a Holy God for a scrutinizing investigation (Romans 14:10,11). The English term "judgment seat" has a Greek origin, *bema seat*. The runners' track in Athens, Greece, contained thousands of seats. However, there was one seat differing from the rest in that it was elevated. The judge of the contest, who sat there, had no obstructions to mar his view. He could see every

movement clearly. This pictures the God of holiness elevated upon His throne watching the Christian's race of
life (2 Corinthians 16:9; Jeremiah 16:7; Hebrews 4:13).
God is keeping records for the day when *we must all
appear before the judgment seat of Christ that everyone
may receive the things done in his body, according to that
he hath done* (2 Corinthians 5:10). We cannot live for the
flesh and self and hear Christ say in that day, "Well
done, thou good and faithful servant." There must be a
battle fought and won. Rewards must be earned and
scars must be traded for crowns. Paul, who *bore in his
body the marks* [scars] *of the Lord Jesus* (Galatians 6:17)
was *pressing toward the mark for the prize of the high
calling of God in Christ Jesus* (Philippians 3:14). Salvation was already his as a gift, but only works of
self-denial, hardship, suffering, and perhaps death
could bring him the prize or crown to lay at Jesus' feet
(Revelation 4:10,11).

God will also investigate the motives behind one's
works. If there is an iota of self-glorification behind any
act of service, the rewards will be sparse . . . if any (Matthew 6:1-6,16-19; 1 Corinthians 3:11-15; 4:5).

Scriptural facts concerning the Bema Seat:

1. This judgment is only for the people of God . . . those
who have erected service or works upon the foundation
of the Lord Jesus Christ.

2. All of God's people present some form of "works" to
Christ at the Bema Seat.

3. Though all worked to some degree, a difference in
quantity and quality is observed . . . gold, silver, and precious stones versus wood, hay, and stubble.

4. The difference is tested by purging fires.

5. The disintegrated ashes of wood, hay, and stubble
bring sorrow and loss (1 Corinthians 3:15). While
eternal life is freely bestowed upon all who believe as a
gift apart from works (Romans 6:23) and cannot be forfeited, rewards and crowns can be earned and lost,
accumulated and liquidated. A day of addition and subtraction is coming at the Rapture.

6. Quality works, performed for the glory of God to win the souls of men — gold, silver, precious stones — will earn crowns for all eternity. These crowns will then be placed at the feet of Christ as an eternal memorial of one's lifetime of service (Revelation 4:10,11).

Some will be ashamed before Him at His coming (1 John 2:28; 2 Peter 1:11). They will have nothing but ashes to lay at Christ's feet. Thank God one can confess failure, rededicate his life, and make a new start immediately. Then such will hear Him say, "Well done, thou good and faithful servant."

KING OF KINGS, LORD OF LORDS K

KEYS OF THE KINGDOM (See Kingdom of Heaven, Keys of)

KINGS OF THE EAST

The word "kings" pictures the leaders of troops. Palestine will be invaded by a great army coming from beyond the Euphrates known as the forces of *the kings of the east* (Revelation 16:12). This represents a great alliance of powers that challenges the authority of the Beast. There will be a miraculous drying up of the river in order that they may cross unhindered.

KING OF THE NORTH

Usually considered to be the Gog of Rosh or Russia, chief prince out of the North (Ezekiel 38,39) (see Armageddon).

KING OF THE SOUTH

Usually considered to be the king of Egypt (Daniel 11) (see Armageddon).

KING OF KINGS, LORD OF LORDS

We have prayed for almost 2,000 years . . . "Thy kingdom come, Thy will be done on earth as it is in heaven." When the Lord Jesus Christ returns to earth in Revelation 19:11-16, He comes as King of Kings! That is the fulfillment of the prayer. Is it near? When will He come as King? What occurs when He arrives?

The Antichrist will have gathered his allies to destroy the Jews and to battle the Lord. Armageddon will have begun. The enemies of the Lord will not be disappointed because Christ appears with His armies (Revelation 19:14). Upon winning at Armageddon, Christ judges the nations and destroys the wicked (Matthew 25:31-46). The beast (Antichrist) and False Prophet are cast into the Lake of Fire (Revelation 19:20). Satan is bound for 1,000 years (Revelation 20:1-3) and the long awaited Millennium begins. When Christ reigns as King of Kings and Lord of Lords in His kingdom, 1,000 years of peace issues out of the city of peace, Jerusalem, the capitol of the world (see Revelation 19,20).

KINGDOM AGE (See Millennium)

KINGDOM, CHILDREN (or sons) OF

By their birth, the Jews believe they have a right to the privileges of the kingdom (Matthew 8:12; 13:38). Although the Jews believe this is their birthright, Christ said it would take faith to be true sons of the kingdom. The parable of the tares may indicate that the believers of the Church Age are the true sons of the kingdom . . . whether Jew or Gentile.

The Lord predicts that many from among the Gentiles will be saved but that most from among the Israelites, the natural sons of the kingdom, will reject their Messiah and be cast into outer darkness (Matthew 8:12). Later in history, when the Messiah appears, all Israel is saved and becomes children of the kingdom (Romans 11:26-28).

KINGDOM OF GOD also *KINGDOM OF HEAVEN*

A comparison of these terms in Matthew and related gospel passages, seems to indicate they are used interchangeably. However, although this distinction is not an integral part of Dispensationalism, many Dispensationalists make a distinction between them. Kingdom of heaven is applied to the earthly, millennial kingdom (Millennium), while the kingdom of God is applied to the eternal, spiritual kingdom. Others apply the kingdom of God to those who are truly saved and the kingdom of heaven only to professing Christians. While these terms are not synonymous, they are used interchangeably. What distinctions there are, are not in the words themselves but in the context as both of these terms are used to designate the millennial kingdom, the spiritual kingdom, and the mystery form of the kingdom.

KINGDOM OF HEAVEN, KEYS OF **K**

KINGDOM OF GOD WITHIN YOU

When the Pharisees asked Christ when the kingdom of God should come (Luke 17:20,21), He said it was "within you," or "in your midst." He was saying that in the person of himself, Christ, the King of Israel, it was already in their midst. All Israel had to do to receive the kingdom was to repent and acknowledge Christ as Messiah and King . . . which they refused to do. Thus, the Age of Grace began postponing the coming kingdom.

KINGDOM OF HEAVEN

A term found only in the Book of Matthew, quoting Daniel's prophecy of the kingdom (see Kingdom of God).

KINGDOM, GOSPEL OF

This is John the Baptist's message: The good news that Messiah is about to set up the kingdom (Matthew 3:1,2; 4:23; 9:35; 24:14). Jesus preached the same message (Matthew 4:23) but was rejected. The same gospel will be preached by 144,000 Jewish missionaries in all the earth during the Tribulation (Matthew 24:14; Revelation 7:4-8) (see Kingdom Postponed).

KINGDOM OF HEAVEN, KEYS OF

A key is a symbol of access to that from which one is otherwise locked out of (Luke 11:52). It certainly doesn't refer to the Church or to opening the door of salvation or heaven. It may refer to the whole sphere of Christian profession or to the future millennial kingdom.

If it means the sphere of Christian profession, then the "keys of the kingdom of heaven" represents the authority which Christ gave to Peter to open the kingdom to the Jews (Acts 2:14), to the Samaritans (Acts 8:14-17), and to the Gentiles (Acts 10:34-46).

If it means the millennial kingdom, then it refers to the future, when the kingdom will be established on earth. Then, in this future view, Christ promises Peter a high position in the coming earthly kingdom.

KINGDOM POSTPONED

This is an act of Christ who deferred or postponed the kingdom after the Jews rejected His genuine offer as the King while He was on earth. According to the dispensationalist interpretation, Christ, during the early part of His ministry on earth, was making a sincere and genuine offer of the millennial kingdom to Israel. The last attempt came as He rode into Jerusalem at the triumphal entry to elicit an official decision on the part of the nation (Mark 8:31). Of course He knew what would happen but He had to present himself as Messiah and be rejected to fulfill Old Testament prophecy (Isaiah 8:14; 53:1-3; Matthew 23:37-39). So the kingdom was delayed, not to be realized until after the Tribulation. At that time, Israel will accept Christ as her Messiah (see Israel, Conversion of), and will enjoy all the blessings promised to her in the covenants.

KNOWLEDGE INCREASED (See Signs)

LAKE OF FIRE

The final place of punishment and torment for all those who reject Christ (Revelation 19:20; 20:10,14,15). Those consigned there are all whose names are not in the Book of Life (Revelation 20:15), along with worshipers of Antichrist (Revelation 14:9,10), as well as the Antichrist and the False Prophet (Revelation 19:20), the devil (Revelation 20:10; Matthew 24:42), and the devil's angels (Matthew 25:41; Revelation 19:20; 20:10). They are all forever separated from God (2 Thessalonians 1:9).

The Lake of Fire is described in Scripture as a place *where their worm dieth not* (Mark 9:44), as a place of *outer darkness* (Matthew 8:12), as a place of *everlasting fire* (Matthew 18:8), where *the smoke of their torment ascendeth* (Revelation 14:11), and where the *second death occurs* (eternal separation from God) (Revelation 20:14) in *fire and brimstone* (Revelation 21:8).

LAMB, LAMB OF GOD

John the Baptist introduced Jesus Christ as the "Lamb of God" which *taketh away the sin of the world* (John 1:29). John knew that Isaiah described Christ in prophecy as a "lamb brought to the slaughter," prophesying the Crucifixion centuries before the fact" (Isaiah 53:1-6). Revelation 13:8 tells us He was the Lamb *slain from the foundation of the world* in the foreknowledge of God. Thus, Jesus Christ became the sacrificial Lamb predicted in the Old Testament, shedding His blood for the remission of sins (Hebrews 9:22,28). This *blood of Jesus Christ,* [God's] *Son, cleanseth us from all sin* (1 John 1:7). Presently no one can overcome Satan but by the blood of the Lamb (Revelation 12:11). John sees Christ as a lamb on the throne, worthy to be praised because of His sacrifice for our sins and the only One worthy to open "the book," the title deed to the earth (Revelation 5:3,5,9).

LAMB'S BOOK OF LIFE (See Book of Life)

LAMPSTANDS

The seven churches are pictured as seven lampstands. This is significant because believers are the light of the world (Matthew 5:14-16). Sad is the fact that history shows the seven churches often diminished and darkened that light (see Churches).

LAODICEA (See Churches)

LAST HOUR

Equivalent to last days, or last "time" in the King James Version (1 John 2:18).

LAST TIME

Equivalent to last day; in 1 Peter 1:5, the final day of the saint's salvation before the Rapture (see Last Days).

LAST TRUMP (See Trump of God)

LATTER TIMES

The time after the writings of the apostles (1 Timothy 4:1).

LION OF THE TRIBE OF JUDAH (See Jesus Christ, Lord)

LITERAL INTERPRETATION (See Interpretation, Methods of)

LITTLE HORN (See Horns)

LOVE, LACK OF (See Signs)

MARK OF THE BEAST M

MAGOG

It was customary in ancient times for descendants of a man to adopt his name for their tribe. Understanding this, historians and Bible students have been able to trace the movements of some of the tribes and know where their descendants are located today. From Magog are descended the ancient Scythians or Tartars whose descendants predominate in modern Russia (Josephus, book one, chapter 7) (see Russia).

MAN OF SIN (See Antichrist)

MANSIONS (See Jerusalem, New)

MARANATHA

A watch word of first century Christians to express the thought, "Our Lord cometh" (see 1 Corinthians 16:22). Revelation 22:20 expresses the thought, "Even so, come, Lord Jesus."

MARK OF THE BEAST

During the Tribulation, the False Prophet will insist that people loyal to Antichrist wear a mark which will be placed either on their right hand or on their forehead. This must be shown to buy or sell (Revelation 13:16-18), or to transact any business. This mark will consist of either the name of the Beast (Antichrist) or his number, 666 (Revelation 14:11).

It is likely that the Image of the Beast, a forth-coming master computer, will give Antichrist all the information necessary for him to govern the world. Its memory bank will know the number, record, and history of every living person. Perhaps this number would be composed of an international, national, and area computer code plus an individual number, such as one's social security number. The present international computer code is "6" ... it could easily be expanded to "666." The present generation of credit card users should readily understand this concept unknown before.

M MARK OF THE BEAST

At the final judgment of God (Great White Throne), all those who received this mark will be *tormented with fire and brimstone . . . and the smoke of their torment ascendeth up forever and ever* (Revelation 14:11).

MARRIAGE OF THE LAMB

The marriage partners at this glorious event include the Lamb (Christ) (Ephesians 5:25-33) and His Bride (the Church). They have been in heaven during the Tribulation Hour. While earth dwellers suffered judgment, the Bride was being investigated in preparation for the wedding (Revelation 19:7) (see Judgment Seat of Christ). For many, who were unfaithful to Christ during the engagement period (their years of service upon earth), this will be a time of humiliation (1 John 2:28) as every believer will be attired in the wedding garment he made upon earth. The material will be composed of their good deeds that remain after the Judgment Seat has occurred (Revelation 19:7,8). Righteousnesses rather than righteousness is the correct word in this text.

The Bride includes all believers from the Day of Pentecost until the Rapture. All Christians will be presented in one body (or group) as a chaste virgin to Christ (2 Corinthians 11:2). Symbolized as a bride, the Church is clothed in fine white linen (Revelation 19:7,8). The Lord Jesus Christ, himself, is the Bridegroom (Ephesians 5:25-33).

The marriage itself takes place in heaven during the end of the Tribulation period on earth. The phrase, *the marriage of the Lamb is come* (Revelation 19:7), signifies that the Church's union with Christ has been completed (1 Thessalonians 4:17). From this point on, wherever Christ goes, His beloved Bride goes with Him.

MARRIAGE SUPPER OF THE LAMB

Following the marriage, heaven opens and Christ, mounted upon a white horse, begins His descent to earth for Armageddon followed by His Bride, the armies clothed in white linen (Revelation 19:11-14).

The place of the wedding reception (Marriage Supper) is somewhat in question. However, I believe that immediately following the marriage, Christ brings His Bride to earth just before the Millennium begins. Tribulation saints are raised when Christ returns to earth in order that they may be guests at the Marriage Supper of the Lamb (Revelation 4:6).

Old Testament Saints and the "friends" of Christ will also attend this event having been resurrected to participate in the Millennium on earth (Daniel 12:2).

It may be either the last thing that happens before the Millennium, during the 75-day interval, or the first event of the Millennium.

MARTYRS, TRIBULATION

During the Tribulation, a mighty revival will result when 144,000 Jewish evangelists cover the earth with their testimony of faith in Christ. Multitudes will be saved from all nations. The reaction of the world dictator, Antichrist, to those who publicly proclaim the end of his reign and announce the coming kingdom of Christ will be an angry explosion of persecution. Millions will be martyred, sealing their testimonies with blood.

These persecuted saints are not part of the Church, the body of Christ, the Bride of the Saviour already in glory (Revelation 4:1). Revelation 6:9 finds their souls under the altar. In the Old Testament, the altar always referred to the place where blood had been sacrificed. Souls will be saved during the Tribulation Hour the same way souls are saved today . . . through the precious shed blood of the Lord Jesus Christ. Because the believers of the Tribulation Hour proclaim Christ crucified, they lose their lives for the Word of God and the testimony of Jesus.

The spirits of the martyred Tribulation saints cry. They also wear white robes. Spirits cannot cry or wear white robes, so apparently the spirit has a temporary covering (2 Corinthians 5:1). We may not understand everything about the spirit world, but one thing is certain, being in spirit form does not mean unconsciousness. Spirits move, talk, cry, and even wear white robes!

Their cry is one of vengeance for blood. They are not under grace as martyred Stephen was (Acts 7:60). This is a different dispensation, the fulfillment of the hour that David spoke of (Psalm 9:12).

There will be a 75-day interval between Christ's return and the Millennium (Daniel 12:11,12). One of the events that takes place during this time is the resurrection of the Old Testament saints and the Tribulation saints (Job 19:25,26; Isaiah 25:8 26:29; Daniel 12:2; Revelation 11:16-18; 20:4,5) so they might be rewarded, as well as be participants in the Millennium on earth (Daniel 12:2). They are also guests at the Marriage Supper of the Lamb. During the Millennium, the Tribulation martyrs will reign with Christ and the Bride (the Church) (Revelation 20:6).

MESHECH

Meshech is the father of a race mentioned in connection with Tubal, Magog, and other northern nations. Generally speaking, Russia is the modern land of Magog, Tubal, and Meshech. Meshech today is Moscow.

MESSIAH

The Jews missed their Messiah (Christ, Saviour). He walked among them and they did not recognize Him, even though their prophets had described His coming in great detail. Ultimately He will end war and establish a government for Israel and the world (see Prophecy; Jesus Christ, Lord). Midway through the Tribulation, Israel will recognize Jesus Christ as Messiah (see Witnesses, 144,000, Remnant).

MID-TRIBULATIONALISM (See Rapture, Views of)

MILLENNIAL SACRIFICES

There is a problem justifying the restoration of a

MILLENNIAL SACRIFICES **M**

priesthood and the reinstitution of a bloody sacrificial system during the Millennium (Ezekiel 20:40,41; 43:18-46; Zechariah 14:16; Isaiah 56:6-8; 66:21; Jeremiah 33:15-18) with the fact that Christ *suffered once for sins, the just for the unjust, that He might bring us to God* (1 Peter 3:18). Thus the following material to elucidate the reinstitution.

The form of worship in the Millennium will bear a strong similarity to the old Aaronic order. When Israel is converted under Jehovah, their God, He will bless them as Israel, not as Christians. When Ezekiel's visions shall be accomplished, it will be the reign of Jehovah-Jesus on earth, and the distinction of Israel from the Gentiles will again be resumed . . . for blessing under the New Covenant, not under the Law. The millennial system is marked by omissions from the Aaronic order that make the two systems different. Yet, the Millennial Age will not see the re-establishment of Judaism as such.

The system to be inaugurated in the Millennial (Kingdom) Age will be a new order that will replace the Levitical order. The whole concept of the New Covenant of Jeremiah 31 envisions an entirely new order after the passing of the old.

Concerning the sacrifices:

1. Nowhere is it stated that they are offered for salvation from sin. The only way it can be held that the sacrifices will be redemptive in the Millennium is to hold that they were so in the Old Testament and that would be a clear contradiction of the whole New Testament (Hebrews 10:4). Old Testament sacrifices repeatedly looked forward to the Lamb of God who would take away the sins of the world. They were insufficient of themselves and picture what was to come when Christ would die on the cross (Hebrews 10:10-12).

2. The sacrifices will be memorial in character. It is not sacrifices rendered to obtain salvation, but sacrifices in view of accomplished salvation . . . as the institution of the Lord's Supper in the church was a

M MILLENNIAL SACRIFICES

memorial, not meant to obtain salvation.

During this present age, God's people worship at His table, with the bread and wine as the memorial of His sacrifice. It is in retrospect. We look back at the cross. We show forth His death "till He comes." Then this memorial will end forever. Never again will the Lord's Supper be kept after the saints of God have left the earth to be with Him in glory (1 Corinthians 13:10).

The resumed sacrifices will be the memorial of the cross during the kingdom reign of Christ and constantly remind the people of earth of Him who died for Israel, who paid the redemption price for all creation.

We see fulfillment of the Davidic Covenant, which was eternal and unconditional, governing God's future dealing with Israel, not the Mosaic, which was temporal and conditional, governing man's relation to God.

MILLENNIUM

Millennium means 1,000 years and refers to the kingdom of Christ on earth. This era, foretold by all the prophets, will be a time of peace among people and nations. War will be but a relic of the past. Jerusalem, known for war, bloodshed, and international tensions, will at last become the city of peace and the capitol of the world. The Prince of Peace will rule from David's throne and the promises given to Mary concerning Jesus will be fulfilled (Luke 1:32,33; Isaiah 9:6,7).

Peace will come to Israel and to the world. But it will not come through military might or treaties. Christ will come bringing peace. When the governments of earth have finally fallen, the Messiah of Israel, the Saviour of men, will set up His kingdom (Daniel 2:44). Satan will be bound for 1,000 years (Revelation 20:1-3). There will be persons with mortal bodies and persons with glorified bodies on earth during this time. Those who survived the Tribulation Hour and who have not been condemned in the judgment of the nations (Matthew 25:31-46) are allowed to enter the Millennium in their mortal bodies and will have prolonged lives. They, along with the millions of babies born during this time, will live for the entire 1,000 years of Christ's reign. If, at the end of this time, they did not rebel with Satan and had accepted Jesus as their Saviour, they will live on eternally.

Their immortal lives will not be spent in glorified bodies but in human bodies eternally preserved through partaking of the tree of life. They will retain perfect health and not experience aging because of the leaves of the trees that grow for the healing of the nations (Revelation 22:2).

The Millennium will bring peace in the world of nature. All of God's creation suffers as a result of the fall of man and will be restored at this time (Romans 8:20-23). Nature will cooperate with man again (Genesis 3:17,18) productivity will return, (Zechariah 8:12), earthquakes, tornadoes, floods, etc., will be absent. Even the animal world will be at peace with man and each other (Isaiah 11:6-8). All economic conflict will be swept away. Oppression and strikes will be unknown with food and housing for all (Isaiah 65:21-23). There will be religious peace with Jews and Gentiles worshipping the Lord together (Isaiah 11:9,10) and the Jews will be at peace in their own land (Ezekiel 36:24-27). All this will happen because the Kingdom Age (Millennium) will be characterized by the fullness of the Spirit (Joel 2:28,29) more than in any previous dispensation. It is evident that all believers will be indwelt by the Holy Spirit in the Millennium even as they are in the present age (Ezekiel 36:27; 37:14; Isaiah 11:2,3; Jeremiah 31:33). No unsaved person will enter the Millennium (the Jews as a nation will have recognized and accepted Christ as Messiah during the Tribulation period and the Gentiles will have experienced conversion prior to admission also (Isaiah 16:5; 18:7; 19:19-21,25; 23:18; 55:5,6; 56:6-8; 60:3-5; 61:8,9; Jeremiah 3:17; 16:19-21; Amos 9:11; Obadiah 17-21).

Earth's motto will be *holiness unto the Lord* (Zechariah 14:20,21). Those reigning with Christ during this time are the returning saints (the Church, the Bride of Christ, Jude 14; Revelation 19:14), the resurrected Old Testament saints (Daniel 12:2), and the raised Tribulation saints (Revelation 20:4). Each group, saved during different dispensations of time, has different duties to perform. The Church is the Bride of Christ and enjoys the 1,000-year honeymoon upon earth reigning with Him (Revelation 20:4; 1 Peter 2:9; Revelation 1:6). The 144,000 serve as accompanying bodyguards for the Lamb and His Bride (Revelation 14:4). The Gentiles saved during the Tribulation will be serving in the glorious temple described in Ezekiel 40-48 and waiting on Christ and His Bride (Revelation 7:15) (see Millennium, Government of).

Terms synonymous with Millennium:

Kingdom of heaven (Matthew 5:10)

The regeneration (Matthew 19:28)

The last day (John 6:40)

The times of refreshing (Acts 3:21)

The restitution of all things (Acts 3:21)

The day of Christ (1 Corinthians 1:8; 2 Corinthians 1:14; Philippians 2:16)

The world to come (Hebrews 2:5)

MILLENNIUM, GOVERNMENT OF

The government will be a theocracy, with Messiah, the Lord Jesus Christ, ruling as King (Daniel 7:13,14; Isaiah 49; Luke 1:32; 22:29) as a son of David (Matthew 1:20; Luke 1:27). Humanly speaking, our Lord's position as son of David was established through Joseph, who adopted him (Luke 3:23; Acts 2:30; 13:22,23,33; Hebrews 7:14; Romans 1:3; Revelation 5:5; 22:16). However, Mary was also of David's descent.

Succession in the kingly line was not altogether by birth, but by appointment.

There is a question as to whether the Lord Jesus Christ will exercise the government over Palestine directly or indirectly through a regent, even David himself (Isaiah 55:3,4; Jeremiah 30:9; 33:15,17,20,21;

Ezekiel 34:23,24; 37:24,25; Hosea 3:5; Amos 9:11).

Nobles and governors will reign under David (Jeremiah 30:21; Isaiah 32:1; Ezekiel 45:8,9). Matthew 19:28 states that 12 disciples will rule over the 12 tribes of Israel, indicating there will be other subordinate rulers administering the government.

There will be even smaller subdivisions of authority (Luke 19:12-28) awarded for faithfulness (Isaiah 40:10; Zechariah 3:7). Judges will be raised up (Zechariah 3:7; Isaiah 1:26). Their authority will demonstrate the theocratic power of Christ to rule with inflexible righteousness and justice (Isaiah 11:3-5), to rule in the fullness of the Spirit (Isaiah 11:2,3), and to rule universally (Daniel 7:14,27). Any outbreak of sin will be dealt with summarily (Isaiah 11:4).

MILLENNIUM, VIEWS OF

Amillennialism states that there is no Millennium. Its advocates deny Isaiah 11:7 and scores of other Old Testament texts. They symbolize and figuratize texts like Isaiah 35:4,5.

Post-millennialism says that Christ will come after the 1,000-year period is completed. They believe the world will become better and better until perfection is achieved. Then Christ will come and take over. Second Timothy 3:13 states just the opposite. Dominion theology is the new label for this belief.

Pre-millennialism (our position): The literal return of Christ will precede the Millennium, 1,000 years of peace on earth under the rule of Jesus Christ, the King of Kings (see Millennium, Kingdom Age).

MOON (See Signs)

MYSTERY

A truth, previously hidden, now made known by revelation of God (Romans 16:25,26; Ephesians 3:3,5; 1 Corinthians 15:51; Colossians 1:26).

M MYSTERY BABYLON

MYSTERY BABYLON (See Babylon)

MYSTERY OF INIQUITY

This is the unmasking of the devil's plan to overthrow the law of God and establish his own rule. This mystery of lawlessness has not been revealed before and was beyond comprehension apart from God's desire to inform us. It is already at work in this world (2 Thessalonians 2:7) (see Signs).

That "man of sin" (2 Thessalonians 2:3) and "man of lawlessness" (see Antichrist) are the same Greek word. He is tied in closely with the mystery of iniquity. Although the man of lawlessness has not yet been revealed, the mystery of lawlessness, which is another way of referring to the spirit of Antichrist, is already at work through the antichrists already present and working (1 John 2:18; 4:3).

NEBUCHADNEZZAR'S DREAM

God gave a preview of the future to a Gentile king who had taken the Jews captive. History has proved the accuracy of that assessment. Fulfillment of the greater part of it has already taken place and the stage is set for the remainder to develop (Daniel 2:28).

The dream is found in Daniel 2:31-35. It is of an image of a man with a head of gold, breast and arms of silver, midsection and thighs of brass, legs of iron, and feet that were part iron and part clay. Its interpretation is veiled without Daniel's explanation. It is understood now by those familiar with the history of the rise and fall of Gentile empires from that day to this and it is intriguing in its implications for the endtime.

The head of gold represented Nebuchadnezzar, whose power in the Babylonian Empire was absolute. Two nations, represented by the arms of silver (the Medes and the Persians) cause the fall of Babylon. The belly and thighs of brass was the Grecian Empire, headed by Alexander the Great. The legs of iron symbolized the Roman Empire . . . why two legs? At one time, it was divided with headquarters in both Rome and Constantinople. The feet of the image, part iron and part clay, spoke of the revival of the Roman Empire in the last days in a deteriorated form with the ten toes representing ten leaders of that coming European federation. The great stone cut out of the mountain that fell on the feet of the image and destroyed it, represents the coming kingdom of Christ that will be established upon His return to earth. He will come when the final stage of the image is developed. We are at that point in history and there can be no doubt that closing time is near (Daniel 2:44,45) (see Ten Nation Conspiracy).

Nearly 40 years later, Daniel was given a vision that confirmed and further explained Nebuchadnezzar's dream (see Daniel's Vision; Beasts, Four).

NEW HEAVEN, NEW EARTH

After this present heaven (surrounding atmosphere)

and earth are renovated at the end of the Millennium, God will create a new heaven and a new earth (Isaiah 65:17; 66:22; 2 Peter 3:13; Revelation 21:1). Israel's covenants guarantee them a nation forever with a king and spiritual blessings unending. Therefore, there must be a place for them to live. The creation of this new earth and heavens is the final act anticipating the eternal kingdom of God (2 Peter 3:13). The eternal destiny of the church saints is related more to a Person (Christ) than to a place. The place is important (see Jerusalem, New; Heaven), but is overshadowed by the Person into whose presence the believer is taken (John 14:3; Colossians 3:4; 1 Thessalonians 4:16,17; 1 John 3:2).

NOAH, DAYS OF (See Signs)

NORTHERN CONFEDERACY (See Gog and Magog)

NUCLEAR WAR (See Days of Lot, Babylon)

NUMBER OF THE BEAST, 666

When Antichrist sets up his one-world government, it appears he will set up a world computer system which will keep track of every person on earth, giving them a number. The number will be "666" (Revelation 13:16-18). As a result, we are encouraged to "count" (compute) the number of the Beast in this reference. Many theories have sprung up through recent years attempting to compute this number. The Bible seems to indicate that the number six is the number of man (Revelation 13:18; the day he was created, etc.). There definitely is numerological meaning within Scripture.

OCCULTISM (See Signs)

OLD TESTAMENT SAINTS

In Old Testament times, Israelites were given the hope of resurrection (Isaiah 26:19,20; Daniel 12:1-3,13; Hosea 13:14; Job 19:25-27), hope of individual judgment and reward (Isaiah 40:10; Ezekiel 11:21; 20:33-44 22:17-22; Daniel 12:3; Zechariah 3:7; 13:9; Malachi 3:16-18; 4:1), and promised blessings in the new heaven and new earth (Isaiah 65:17,18; 66:22; Hebrews 11:10). Those who heeded the message of God died and went to a place called Paradise. This area was evacuated after Christ's death (Ephesians 4:8-10) (see Hades, Abraham's Bosom). Their spirits are now in the third heaven with Christ (2 Corinthians 12:2). They are not part of the Church. The Church began to be formed on the Day of Pentecost and will be completed at the Rapture.

They are called saints because of their position "in Christ." They were saved by looking forward in faith to a coming Messiah, the Saviour, just as people are saved today by looking back in faith to the Saviour.

Their bodies will be resurrected at the conclusion of the Tribulation so that they, along with the raised Tribulation saints, might be participants in the Millennium here on earth (Revelation 20:4-6; Daniel 12:2). They will also be guests at the Marriage Supper of the Lamb.

OLIVET DISCOURSE

On the Mount of Olives, Christ gave an outline of Israel's future up to the Millennium (Matthew 24-25; Mark 13; Luke 21).

There are four basic views of interpretation:
1. All has been fulfilled in the past
2. All is to be fulfilled in the Church Age
3. All will be fulfilled in the Tribulation and introductory times of the Millennium (I teach this view — JVI)
4. Part has been fulfilled in Jewish history, part will be fulfilled in the Tribulation

O OLIVET DISCOURSE

Although there are many variations among Dispensationalists, the following is representative:

Matthew 24:4-8: First half of the Tribulation

Matthew 24:9-26: Second half of the Tribulation

Matthew 24:27-31: Second Coming of Christ (Revelation)

Matthew 24:32-51: Practical applications

Matthew 25:1-30: Judgment of Israel

Matthew 25:31-46: Judgment of Nations (Gentiles)

ONE HUNDRED FORTY-FOUR THOUSAND (See Witnesses, Remnant)

OVERCOMERS (See Tribulation Saints, Martyrs)

PARADISE (See Hades)

PAROUSIA (See Christ, Coming of)

PARTIAL RAPTURE THEORY (See Rapture, Views of)

PAST-TRIBULATION

This term comes from J. Barton Payne, who believes the Tribulation period is already past, fulfilled in history, and Christ could come at any time. This is also the basic theory of the Seventh Day Adventists.

PEACE

Real peace can only come when the Prince of Peace returns. Until then, there will be no lasting peace on earth. The crescendo of peace rhetoric that has already begun is but a sign of end-time destruction (1 Thessalonians 5:3). Talk of peace will be increasingly the order of the day. Western nations, the United Nations, and the communist world, acting together and unilaterally with behind-the-scenes bargaining and diplomatic arm-twisting, will make the push for peace irresistible. But peace will not come easily or permanently to the Middle East and the world.

Jerusalem itself presents an almost insurmountable obstacle to peace. The Jewish desire for peace has waited long and weathered many storms since the dispersion.

The Lord Jesus Christ is the Prince of Peace (Isaiah 9:6). Seven years before Christ returns to set up His kingdom of peace, Satan, the counterfeiter and super deceiver (1 Thessalonians 2:4), will cause the Antichrist to present himself as the Messiah (or Christ) and he will be accepted! He will come into prominence and power by presenting a "world peace program" to the nations. The contracts are then signed and confirmed in Daniel 9:27.

Since Israel became a nation, she has not dwelled safely. Now comes an hour of peace and the world says,

P PEACE

"Utopia! The world leader is here. No more war. Peace! Peace!" But the Antichrist's peace contract lasts only 42 months (Daniel 9:27). Although he signs a peace contract of seven years (84 months), he breaks it at the halfway point (42 months). Then Russia marches to the Middle East (Ezekiel 38:11). The following 42 months will not see a moment's peace until Christ returns and brings in the Millennium. When He reigns (Isaiah 9:6), mankind will beat their swords into plowshares and their spears into pruning hooks in a day of incomparable rejoicing. Peace at last . . . for 1,000 years (Isaiah 2:4) (see Millennium). (See also Isaiah 11:6-9; 32:17,18; 33:5,6; 54:13; 55:12; 60:18; 65:25; 66:12; Ezekiel 28:26; 34:25,28; Micah 4:2,3; Zechariah 19:10).

PERDITION (See Hell)

PERGAMOS (See Churches)

PERSECUTIONS (See Holocausts, Martyrs)

PESTILENCE (See Signs)

PHILADELPHIA (See Churches)

PLAN FOR THE AGES (Prophetic Clock)

(See Nebuchadnezzar's Dream and Daniel's Vision of Seventy Weeks.) The Jewish people do not realize that the prophetic clock came to a halt when they rejected their Messiah, who came right on schedule (see Jesus Christ, Lord; Messiah). One week of years is left unfulfilled until the Age of Grace is over (see Church Age, Times of the Gentiles) and the Church raptured (see Rapture). Israel will then again become the object of God's special dealing and the final seven years of Daniel's vision will be counted off in the world's most terrible time, the Tribulation period.

The prophetic clock ticks on during the seven years, as God's plan for the ages continues with the Tribulation

period ending in the Battle of Armageddon and the return of Christ, who defeats all opposing armies. Satan is also bound for 1,000 years. Christ then judges the nations and the rebels are punished (Matthew 25:31-46). Next is the millennial or 1,000-year reign of Christ. After this, Satan is loosed out of his prison and goes forth to deceive the nations globally (Revelation 20:7-9 (see Rebellion, Satan's). It is short-lived and he is cast into the Lake of Fire (Revelation 20:9). Next on the agenda is the Great White Throne Judgment for unbelievers of all ages (Revelation 20:11-15). Finally the destruction of the old earth and heavens occurs (2 Peter 3:10,11; Matthew 24:35) and a creation of the new earth and heavens ensues (Revelation 21:1,2,10; Isaiah 65:17) (see Chronology).

PLEASURE (See Signs)

POST-MILLENNIALISM (See Millennium, Views of)

POST-TRIBULATIONISTS (See Rapture, Views of)

POWERLESS CHURCH (See Signs)

POWERS OF HEAVEN SHAKEN (See Signs)

PRE-MILLENNIALISM (See Millennium, Views of)

PRE-TRIBULATIONISTS (See Rapture, Views of)

PREY

When Russia invades Israel, it is to take a spoil and a prey (Ezekiel 38:11,12). Russia is after the spoil while the Arabs come for the prey. The prey is the people themselves. For thousands of years the Jews have been the prey of persecutors. In this war, the Arab nations will be allies of Russia and their primary purpose will be to take a prey . . . Israel.

PRIDE (See Signs)

PROPHECY

Prophecy is history written in advance. Prophecy's accuracy hinges upon the dependency of the one who made it. Bible prophecy is God's description of future events (Acts 15:18). God's Word contains 10,385 predictions and each one has been or will be fulfilled in the minutest of details. God's Word has proven itself by not failing in one small point concerning Christ's first coming. Prophecy concerning His Second Coming is also being fulfilled and skeptics must forever admit their shortsightedness (Romans 3:4). He *will* come again (Acts 1:11) (see Christ, Prophecies Fulfilled).

PROPHECY, GIFT OF

A temporary gift of the Holy Spirit during the apostolic church days in which a believer received a message directly from God (1 Corinthians 12:10; 13:2,8).

PROPHET

A man, chosen by God, inspired to speak forth God's message to reveal the future to man. A prophet is a forth teller and a foreteller. He speaks for God through direct communication (Exodus 33:11; Numbers 12:8), through dreams (Numbers 12:6; Daniel 7:1), or through visions (Daniel 7:1; Hosea 12:10). Old Testament verification of a prophet included a judgment as to whether he spoke according to the Law and to the testimony (Isaiah 8:20) and whether his prophecy came to pass (Deuteronomy 18:22).

It seems that Enoch was the first prophet (Jude 14). A school of prophets was founded under Samuel (1 Samuel 10:5; 19:20; 2 Kings 2:3,5; 4:38; 6:1).

RAINBOW

Christ, in His deity, is usually surrounded by a cloud (Psalm 97:2; Exodus 16:9,10; 40:34,38; Matthew 17:5; Acts 1:9; Luke 21:27; Revelation 1:7; 10:1). When God made a covenant with Noah, He placed a rainbow in the cloud as a symbol of His mercy. The rainbow pictures mercy in the midst of judgment. Who but the Lord could wear it (Revelation 10:1, 4:3)? Christ is often pictured as One who has a shining face as unto the sun. In fact, Saul of Tarsus met this One whose countenance is light on the Damascus turnpike (Acts 9:3). The combination of clouds and sun often produces rainbows, a "sign" or symbol that He keeps His Word (Genesis 9:13).

RAPTURE

There are two stages or phases within the process of the Second Coming — the Rapture and the Revelation — and these are separated by a seven-year period of time.

The Rapture is the next occurrence on God's calendar and is the literal, visible, and bodily return of Christ in the heavenlies. He shall return as He left (Acts 1:9-11). One can easily know how He departed by studying Luke 24:39. He had a new resurrected body of flesh and bones — a body that could be seen, touched, and fed (vss. 41-43). When He returns in the heavenlies, all believers, dead and living, will also be taken bodily to meet Him in the clouds. We shall be changed as this mortal body puts on immortality and is transformed to be like Jesus' body (1 Corinthians 15:51-54; Psalm 17:15; 1 John 3:2). This happens in a moment, in "the twinkling of an eye."

This event ends the Church Age and ushers in the Tribulation period. The Rapture of the Church involves the resurrection of the Christian dead as well as the exit from earth of all believers living at that time (1 Thessalonians 4:13-18). Regarding the Christian dead, the Bible teaches that the body is asleep in one place (the grave) whereas the soul is alive in another place (heaven). To be "absent from the body" is to be present with the Lord (2 Corinthians 5:8). When Christ returns at the Rapture, He brings those that sleep (are dead) with Him (1 Thessalonians 4:14). How can He bring the dead with Him and still come for the dead (1 Thessalonians 4:16)? The dead are in two places! The souls and spirits are with the Lord, but their bodies are in the grave. Hence Christ brings the dead (souls and spirits) with Him so they may be reunited with their bodies. That is why the dead in Christ rise first.

The return of Christ for His Church is a signless and always imminent event. Even the New Testament writers expected the Lord's return at any moment (Philippians 3:20). All signs of the Lord's return have to do with the coming of Christ to set up His kingdom. They are only indicators of the approaching Rapture because that event precedes the establishment of the kingdom by seven years . . . in fact, we must be raptured so as to return with Him. The moment the Antichrist signs the seven-year peace pact the Tribulation period will begin and a timetable will be evident. Date-setting will now be conclusive and Christ's return will no longer be imminent. It will be exactly 84 months or 2,520 days until Christ returns to establish His kingdom. The Rapture must precede the Tribulation Hour.

The Church is not to be the recipient of wrath. When one considers God's purpose for the Tribulation, it is difficult to place the Bride of Christ into such a horrendous scene. Why should Christ's Bride suffer the judgments of the seven seals, seven trumpets, and seven vials found in Revelation 6,8,9,11,15,16, when the Church cannot be found beyond the third chapter of the Book of Revelation? No, the Tribulation Hour is primarily a time of judgment upon a Christ-rejecting, God-rejecting world — both Jew and Gentile (Ezekiel 20:37,38; Micah 5:15). Paul assured the Thessalonian Christians that they would not go through the Tribulation (1 Thessalonians 5:9). Although the Church is not all it should be, the world is better because the Church is present. The Holy Spirit, working through Christians, holds back the tide of evil sweeping the world. When His influence in this manner is removed at the Rapture, think of the wickedness that shall follow!

During the Tribulation period on earth, the raptured Christians have an appointment with Christ at the Judgment Seat of Christ (2 Corinthians 5:19; Romans 14:10,12).

The word "rapture" does not appear in the Bible. It was coined from the Latin *rapio* or *rapere* to portray the experience of being "snatched away." This is what is going to happen one day soon as the people of God disappear from the earth and immediately meet Christ to stand before the Judgment Seat.

RAPTURE, VIEWS OF

Controversy surrounds the subject of the return of Christ for His Church — whether it is before, during, or after the Tribulation period.

Pre-Tribulation View

This conviction is based on the following:

1. *The promise to the Church in Philadelphia* (Revelation 3:10)

The seven churches of Revelation 2 and 3 represent the professing Church in seven successive epochs from the Day of Pentecost to the time of the Lord's return. Each church fits chronologically into its respective place in history.

The sixth church, "Philadelphia," escapes the Tribulation Hour, but the seventh, "Laodicea" is rejected by Christ. True believers, possessing Christ, are kept from the hour of temptation that immerses our entire planet: "I also will keep thee from (not through) the hour of temptation." *God hath not appointed us to wrath* (1 Thessalonians 5:9).

2. *The case of the 24 elders* (Revelation 4:1)

Many believe the "come up hither" call of Revelation 4:1 pictures the Rapture of the Church prior to the beginning of earth's holocaust.

The 24 elders represent believers of all ages, members

of the royal priesthood (1 Peter 2:9). Revelation 4 and 5 is the direct outcome of the Rapture. The Church is present in heaven and the 24 representatives of God's people are singing about the blood of the Lamb. They are arrayed in white and have received their crowns before the first seal of judgment is broken in Chapter 6. The Church cannot be found in the Book of Revelation during any of the judgments, but is seen returning with the Saviour in Chapter 19 when the Tribulation concludes.

3. *The Holy Spirit, the hinderer, is taken out of the way* (2 Thessalonians 2:7,8)

When the Thessalonican Christians were fearful, thinking that perhaps they were experiencing the Day of the Lord or Tribulation (2 Thessalonians 2:1-5), Paul assured them that it couldn't have come yet because there first had to be a departure from the faith and the Antichrist had to be revealed. He further stated that the Antichrist could not be made manifest until the One who restrains the Antichrist's appearing was removed, namely the Holy Spirit (vss. 7,8).

The Holy Spirit lives in the hearts of believers. Our bodies constitute His temple during the Church Age (1 Corinthians 6:19). Therefore, when He ceases to hinder the appearing of the Antichrist, His temple, the believers, must be removed via the Rapture.

4. *The Tribulation is called "the Time of Jacob's Trouble"* (Jeremiah 30:7; Romans 11:26) *and "Daniel's Seventieth Week"* (Daniel 9)

In history, the first 69 weeks of Nebuchadnezzar's Dream involved Israel (Daniel 9:24). Why wouldn't the seventieth or final week also involve Israel? Why revert to the Church of the Lord Jesus Christ? (see Remnant; Evangelists, 144,000).

Mid-Tribulation View

According to this view, Christians would pass through the first half of the Tribulation but be raptured at the seventh trumpet judgment (see Judgments). This destroys the biblical teaching of imminence.

Partial Rapture View

This position is not concerned with the time of the translation (Rapture) in relation to the Tribulation period, but with the people being raptured. They believe that not all believers will be taken, but only those who are "watching" and "waiting," who have attained some plateau of spiritual standing that makes them ready. This undercuts Christ's atonement which frees the sinner from condemnation and makes him acceptable to God.

The distinction between law and grace is lost, as is the distinction between the Church and Israel when passages intended for Israel are applied to the Church. Nowhere in scriptural teaching on rewards does the Rapture appear as the reward for watching while an undeserving part of the body of Christ is left to suffer through the Tribulation, separated from the rest of the Body. The Body is one and cannot arrive by bits and pieces in heaven (1 Corinthians 12:12,13; Ephesians 5:30).

Remember, after the Rapture, at the Bema Seat, the bad (1 Corinthians 3:15) is judged with the good, and the ashamed are present (1 John 2:28). As far as works go, these couldn't have been worthy or ready.

Post-Tribulation View

This view does not look for Christ to come for His own until after the Tribulation. Therefore, the Church is not looking for "the blessed hope" of the return of Christ, but judgments and horrors of the Tribulation period.

This theory destroys both the doctrine of imminence and the teaching of Dispensationalism. The Rapture is not based on any specific set of signs because it is imminent. The Rapture is connected with eminency while the Revelation is not (see Second Coming). The Rapture takes place in Revelation 4:1, and the signs begin in chapter 6. The signs point to the Revelation, or Christ's return to the earth (Revelation 19:11). This second phase or revelation of Christ is not based on the Bible teaching of imminence. Instead, one can definitely know when Christ's return to earth will transpire by the signs pointing to it in the Book of Revelation, chapters 6-18. The following passages mention Christ's coming for His own without any specific timetable: Acts 1:11; Philippians 3:20; Colossians 3:4; 1 Timothy 6:14; James 5:8; 1 Peter 3:3,4.

REBELLION, SATAN'S

For the duration of the Millennium, Satan has been in the bottomless pit, a temporary prison, chained for ten centuries in order that peace, prosperity, happiness, and holiness may exist on earth. At the end of this time, he is loosed for a little season, leads one final revolt against God, and is subsequently cast into the eternal Lake of Fire where the Beast and False Prophet already are (Revelation 19:20).

One might wonder why Satan is loosed to go out and deceive the nations of the earth again (Revelation 20:7-9). The answer: The children born during the Millennium possess the old Adamic or sin-prone nature. They are the ones who are deceived by Satan and join in his rebellion. This shows the innate wickedness of the human heart. These people have known what it was like to live in peace under Christ! Still, after being in His presence 1,000 years, they rebel.

Satan organizes and leads the insurrection for a brief period of time. Then, fire comes down from God and devours Satan and his followers (Revelation 20:9). Then the devil is cast into the Lake of Fire (vs. 10).

RELIGIOUS SYSTEM, FALSE

The false religious system that prospers during the early part of the reign of Antichrist is described in Revelation 17. This blasphemous, ecclesiastical empire will thrive on pomp and ceremony and will give allegiance to the irreverent final world dictator, the Beast (see Babylon, Religious; Whore; World Church).

Many Jews who do not turn to Christ during the Tribulation will return to Temple worship as in Old Testament times.

Ultimately, however, Antichrist will destroy the false church and take control of Jewish worship, declaring himself to be God and demanding worship from the Jews in their own Temple (Daniel 2:11) (see Abomination of Desolation).

REMNANT (JEWISH), 144,000

The existence of a remnant of Jews is tied to the covenants God made with the nation Israel. The unconditional covenants must have a people to carry out their fulfillment. Even though Israel has often strayed far from the Lord, He has always had a believing remnant. In New Testament times there were always a believing, expectant nucleus to whom the promises were reaffirmed. Presently a remnant of Israel are turning to Messiah, Jesus and receiving His salvation.

Shortly after the Rapture, there will be another remnant of Jews who turn to Christ. These converted Jews are called "servants of God" and they are extremely successful in ministering to others. Not long after this elect group is announced by John, he describes a great multitude from all nations who have been converted to Christ as a result of their labor and who are willing to prove their faith through martyrdom.

RESTRAINER

The Holy Spirit will continue to restrain the working of lawlessness until the Rapture, when His restraining power will be removed (Believers) (2 Thessalonians 2:6,7) (see Mystery of Iniquity; Holy Spirit).

RESURRECTION

There shall be a resurrection of the dead, both of the just and unjust (Acts 24:15). All unbelievers of all ages will be resurrected for the Great White Throne Judg-

R RESURRECTION

ment (Revelation 20:11-15; John 5:28,29; Acts 24:15; 1 Corinthians 15:22-24). Their bodies will come forth from land and sea and their souls will come from Hades (or hell). Then body, soul, and spirit are reunited to stand before God (see Hell).

It will be a solemn scene as unregenerate mankind comes face-to-face with God. Every transgressor is present: presidents and paupers, small and great, rich and poor. As the unsaved stand before a Holy God, the books are opened and a totally accurate record of every wicked deed ever committed is exposed in detail (Hebrews 4:13).

RESURRECTION BODY (See Bodies, Glorified)

RESURRECTION, FIRST (Resurrection Unto Life)

Resurrection of all saints of all ages (Revelation 20:4-6; John 5:28,29; 1 Corinthians 15; Job 19:25,26):

Christ, "the firstfruits" (1 Corinthians 15:20)

Church-age saints at Rapture (1 Thessalonians 4:13-18)

Israel and Old Testament saints at the close of the Tribulation (Isaiah 26:19; Daniel 12:1-3)

RESURRECTION UNTO DAMNATION

Resurrection of all unsaved dead at the close of the Millennium (Revelation 20:5,11-14; John 5:28,29). All these will appear before the Great White Throne Judgment and be cast into the Lake of Fire (see Great White Throne Judgment).

RETURN, CHRIST'S (See Revelation; Second Coming)

REVELATION

There are two stages or phases within the process of the Second Coming — the Rapture and the Revelation — and these events are separated by a seven-year period of time, the Tribulation.

The second phase is described as "the Revelation." "Revelation" is but a coined word (His revealing), picturing the truth it describes. Just when it looks hopeless for the Jews, Christ appears in the clouds, riding a white horse and accompanied by great armies of His saints to finish off the armies of the world at Armageddon. Revelation 19:11-16 gives us a glimpse of that momentous event when He is revealed as King of Kings and Lord of Lords. *Every eye shall see him* (Revelation 1:7).

Unlike the Rapture, the exact date of Christ's Revelation may be known. When the Antichrist persuades Israel to sign his international peace contract, one can begin marking days. The Battle of Armageddon and Christ's return to the earth will be exactly 2,520 days from the date of this signing (see Second Coming).

REVELATION, PROGRESSIVE

To progress from truth to a greater expression of the same truth. God reveals more of himself and His divine plan from the early books of Scripture progressively onward. Looking back on Genesis 3:15, we see now the whole truth of God's plan of salvation. It is impossible to progress from error to truth. Error must be forsaken and a new start made with truth.

REWARDS OF RIGHTEOUSNESS

One is neither saved nor kept by works (2 Timothy 1:9), but good works naturally follow salvation (Ephesians 2:10).

There is a system of balances found in the Scriptures when it comes to rewards, but not to salvation, which is a gift (Romans 6:23). These works will be weighed on God's scales and put through judgmental fire. Thus, a system of addition and subtraction can be found at the Judgment Seat of Christ. Quality works, performed for the glory of God to win the souls of men when tested and found genuine, will earn crowns for the faithful for all eternity. They are likened to gold, silver, and precious stones (1 Corinthians 3:12-15). Eternal life is freely bestowed upon all who believe as a gift apart from works (Romans 6:23), and cannot be forfeited, but crowns can be earned and lost, accumulated and liquidated.

A Christian can accumulate rewards while he is on earth and then lose them before his death or the Rapture by foolish living. These are the consequences of a Christian living in sin (not loss of salvation, but of rewards ... saved "so as by fire" (1 Corinthians 3:15; 2 John 8; Revelation 3:11; 2 Timothy 4:7,8).

At the Judgment Seat of Christ, the Lord Jesus Christ will present a number of "crowns" for specific service:

The *Watcher's Crown* (a Crown of Righteousness), given to all who longingly and desiringly watch for Christ's return (2 Timothy 4:8).

The *Runner's Crown* (an Incorruptible Crown), for all who strive for the mastery by keeping bodily appetites under control and being temperate in all things (1 Corinthians 9:24-27).

The *Shepherd's Crown* (a Crown of Glory) reserved for faithful ministers (1 Peter 5:1-4).

The *Soulwinner's Crown* (a Crown of Rejoicing), for those who bring others to the Saviour (1 Thessalonians 2:19; Psalm 126:5,6; Luke 15:5,6,7,10).

The *Sufferer's Crown* (a Crown of Life), for those who have suffered for the sake of Christ and the gospel (James 1:12; Matthew 5:10-12). It is also given to those who are faithful unto the end (Revelation 2:10).

ROMAN EMPIRE, REVIVED (See Ten Nation Conspiracy)

RUSSIA

Russia will invade Israel from the "north" in the "latter years" (Ezekiel 38:15,16) when the Jews are in their own land.

Students of the Bible have always expected this to happen. The key names in Ezekiel's prophecy are first mentioned in Genesis 10 as sons of Japeth, the son of

Noah. They are Gomer, Magog, Tubal, and Meshech (Genesis 10:1,2). These key verses describe the repopulating of the earth after the Flood. It was customary in ancient times for the descendants of a man to adopt his name for their tribe. Using this system, scholars have furnished the following information:

1. *Magog* — his descendants are the Scythians or Tartars, whose descendants today are found in modern Russia. Scythians were called Magogites by the Greeks 2,000 years ago (Josephus, book one, chapter seven).

2. *Tubal* — his descendants peopled the region south and north of the Black Sea. Tobolsk (the "sk" being the Russian suffix) perpetuates the tribal name and is presently located southwest of Siberia.

3. *Meshech* — his descendants are northern nations mentioned in connection with Tubal and Magog. Meshech is the original name for Moscow.

4. *Rosh* — the word "chief" in Ezekiel 38:3 is "Rosh" in Hebrew. "Behold, I am against thee, O Gog, the Rosh prince of Meshech and Tubal." "Rosh" was the name of the tribe dwelling in the area of the Volga and it is the word for "Russia" today in some languages of the world. The name "Russia" was formed from the ancient name "Rosh" It is clear that Ezekiel was delivering a warning to the Russian prince of Meshech and Tubal. Gog is the prince, Magog his land, the reference to Meshech and Tubal (Moscow and Tobolsk) is a clear mark of identification.

Allies of Russia in that fierce conflict will be Persia (Iran and Iraq), Ethiopia, Libya, Gomer (Eastern Germany and Slovakia), and Togarmah (Turkey). Daniel adds Egypt to the names of nations coming against Israel (Daniel 11:40-44).

The Russians will be pleased to cooperate with the others, knowing that when their military forces overrun the Middle East they will control all the wealth there, including Arab oil. Add to this the mineral wealth of the Dead Sea (two trillion dollars), as well as the wealth being generated in Israel through industry and agriculture. The Arabs will join the attack to take a prey, Israel, while Russia will be invading to take a spoil (Ezekiel 38:11,12).

The Jews will be dwelling securely. It seems likely this security (vs. 11) will come from enacting a treaty with the head of the Western Alliance, or the revived Roman Empire. It is intended to last for seven years (Daniel 9:27) (see Ten Nation Alliance).

It appears that the Russian invasion will come about the middle of the Tribulation period, approximately three and one-half years after signing the treaty. This attack on Israel will be her greatest military blunder ever. Though brief, the conflict will be one of the most destructive in history. Their casualties will be so great that only one-sixth of the fighting force is left after the battle.

Two important developments will follow the defeat of the invaders of Israel:

1. Russia's attack will give Antichrist an excuse for full occupation of Israel under the pretense of protection and will extend his power over the entire world.

2. The divine protection of Israel, prophesied by Ezekiel and proclaimed by the 144,000 evangelists, will turn many Jews to their Messiah, the Lord Jesus Christ.

Russia will be driven back to Siberia (Ezekiel 39:1,2; Joel 2:20) where she will strengthen her forces and return to Israel once again. The scope and intensity of the offensive continues to increase until all nations become involved and are finally gathered together against Israel at Jerusalem (Zechariah 14:2). At that point, the Battle of Armageddon takes place (Revelation 16:16).

SACRIFICES (See Tribulation Sacrifices; Millennial Sacrifice)

SAINTS

A holy person: pious Israelites (Psalm 16:3; 34:9; 89:5,7), all believers saved by turning to Christ, the Lamb of God (1 Corinthians 1:2; Romans 6:3,4; 8:1; Ephesians 1:3).

While it is true that by experience some believers are more holy than others, yet in their position before God, all believers are saints by virtue of what they are "in Christ" (see Old Testament Saints; Tribulation Saints; Martyrs).

SARDIS (See Churches)

SATAN

Satan's rebellion against God's authority began in heaven (Ezekiel 28:12-19; Isaiah 14:12-17). Since his expulsion into the first and second heavens, he has waged a reign of terror upon the earth's inhabitants. He is the great deceiver in charge of fallen angels determined to wreak havoc upon this earth.

When the Holy Spirit has finally relinquished his restraining power at the Rapture, Satan will make his final bid to frustrate God's plan during the Tribulation activities. Satan will unveil two satanically-inspired beasts who come out of the sea and earth. They are Antichrist and the False Prophet.

Satan knows prophecy and he is the great imitator. He will form an unholy trinity. Knowing his time is short, he makes an all-out move to usurp God's position and authority through these two allies, the Antichrist (false saviour) and the False Prophet (false holy spirit). The Antichrist effectively "sets up his kingdom" by political maneuvering (see Ten Nation Conspiracy) and the False Prophet is his religious leader who causes the people of the world to worship the Image of the Beast (Revelation 13:1).

Satan is doomed to defeat by the King of Kings at the Battle of Armageddon, bound in the bottomless pit for 1,000 years during the Millennium, is released, and then, after one last desperate attempt to deceive the nations of the world, is cast into the Lake of Fire prepared for him and his angels (Revelation 20:10; Matthew 25:41).

SCOFFERS (See Signs)

SEA AND WAVES ROARING (See Signs)

SEA OF GLASS

The sea of glass speaks of tranquility. It is calm and stable and typifies:

1. The Church at rest (Revelation 4:6)
2. God's living Word. Solomon's Temple contained a sea of glass, depicting the Word of God, as a means of sanctification.

In Revelation 15:2, it is mixed with fire. This is a beautiful picture of believers standing firmly for Christ under the test of fire, having their feet planted upon the Word of God (1 Peter 1:7).

SEALS (See Judgments)

SECOND ADVENT

The return of the Lord to earth at the close of the Tribulation, also called the Revelation. This event is different than the Rapture (see Second Coming).

SECOND COMING

The happiness of the greatest event in world history has to do with seeing Jesus. When the Lord Jesus Christ returns to earth - His revealing - in Revelation 19, He comes as King of Kings (Revelation 19:16). This happens when the Roman Empire has been revived in the form of a ten

SHEEP AND GOAT NATIONS **S**

There are two stages or phases within the process of the Second Coming — the Rapture and the Revelation — and these events are separated by a seven-year period of time, the Tribulation (see Rapture; Revelation).

SECOND DEATH (See Hell; Lake of Fire)

SEED OF THE WOMAN
This term is taken from Genesis 3:15, referring to some progeny of Eve that would be at enmity with the seed of the serpent, the devil (Isaiah 7:14; Galatians 4:4). Ultimately and specifically, this person is Jesus Christ. Generally, it is true that the serpent's seed has always been at war with the woman's seed. It still continues today.

SELFISHNESS (See Signs)

SERMON ON THE MOUNT
This message, delivered by Christ to His disciples, relates to a kingdom truth primarily concerning repentance, a return to true godliness, and a spiritual keeping of the Law. If the reader is careful not to misapply kingdom truth to the Church Age, this great sermon has value even in the Grace era (2 Timothy 3:16).

SEVENTY WEEKS OF DANIEL (See Daniel's Seventy Weeks)

SHEEP AND GOAT NATIONS
Following Christ's defeat of the opposing armies at Armageddon, the Lord Jesus Christ begins His judgment of the nations (Matthew 25:31-46). First the rebels, or goat nations, are purged to go into judgment and punishment, then those who have been converted (the sheep) by accepting the message that the 144,000 Jews preached during the Tribulation Hour go into the millennial reign of Christ (Revelation 7:14; Acts 2:21).

S SHEEP AND GOAT NATIONS

Individuals who rejected the message are lost, just as any sinner in any dispensation is lost because he rejects the Saviour.

SHEOL (See Hades)

SIGNS OF THE TIMES

In Matthew 24:3, Christ's disciples asked, *What shall be the sign of thy coming, and of the end of the world?* The Saviour then proceeded to describe those world events which would both indicate His return and culminate in the Day of the Lord. He added in Luke 21:28, *And when these things begin to come to pass* [or begin to occur simultaneously], *then look up, and lift up your heads; for your redemption draweth nigh.* These signs of Christ's Second Coming are in evidence worldwide, and increasing both in frequency and intensity.

The actual Second Coming of Christ to the earth is the second phase, the Revelation, or the revealing of Christ. Since He came to earth at His First Advent, He must come to earth at His Second Advent. The Rapture is not Christ's appearance upon earth, but a meeting in the heavenlies (1 Thessalonians 4:17), and intermediary evacuation of believers from earth before the storm (Tribulation). Seven years later, Christ does come to earth, touching down on the Mount of Olives (Zechariah 14:4). The prophetical signs point to Christ's return to earth with His saints at the close of the Tribulation Hour — not to the Rapture. Even if there were not a sign yet in existence, believers could be called home imminently because each of the signs could occur during the seven-year period following the believers' departure.

God has two elect groups upon earth — Israel (Romans 11:28) and the Church (1 Peter 1:2). The signs of Matthew 24 are presented to elect Israel. We know this to be true because of the regard for the Sabbath Day (vs. 20), synagogues (Luke 21:12), and because the setting is Jerusalem (vs. 20). These signs are for Israel who is looking for the return of her King in Revelation 19. They are not signposts for the Rapture. The gospel mentioned in Matthew 24:24 is the gospel of the kingdom that the King is about to return (Revelation 19:16) (see Gospel of the Kingdom).

Although the signs are completely fulfilled after the Christians are gone, we already see the beginnings of every one of these prophecies (Luke 21:28).

Matthew 24 is spoken to Israel rather than the Church. The signs are not pre-Rapture signals but post-Rapture signposts for Israel. They point to the coming of Christ to this earth as King of Kings and Lord of Lords (Revelation 19:11-16). Order my book, *11:59 . . . and Counting!* for a detailed study.

Old Testament Signs of the endtimes:
- Horseless carriages or automobiles (Nahum 2:3,4)
- Airplanes (Isaiah 31:5)
- Desert blossoming as a rose (Isaiah 35:1)
- Alignment of a ten nation western confederacy (Daniel 2,7)
- Knowledge explosion (Daniel 12:4)
- Great increases in travel (Daniel 12:4)

New Testament Signs of the endtimes:
- False Christs and False Prophets (Matthew 24:5,24; 2 Peter 2:1)
- Wars and rumors of wars (Mark 13:7; Matthew 24:6)
- Famines, earthquakes in divers places, pestilences (Luke 21:11)
- Iniquity abounding (Matthew 24:12)
- Gospel of the kingdom preached to all the world (Matthew 24:14)
- Signs in the sun, moon, and stars, sea and waves roaring (Luke 17:26-30; 21:25-27)
- Introduction of evil spirits which control cults and false religions (1 Timothy 4:1,2)

The 19 signs of 2 Timothy 3:1-5, signs within man:
- Lovers of themselves, covetous, boasters, proud, blas-

phemers, disobedient to parents, unthankful, unholy, without natural affection, trucebreakers, false accusers, incontinent (drunkenness, gluttony, deviate sex, drugs), fierce, despisers of those that are good, traitors, heady, highminded, lovers of pleasure more than lovers of God, having a form of godliness, but denying the power thereof.

- Hoarding of gold and silver, and its final demise (James 5:1-3)
- Scoffers mocking the Second Coming of Christ (2 Peter 3:3,4)
- Lethargy and indifference among God's people (Revelation 3:14-16)
- Invention of the atom bomb (2 Peter 3:10)
- Jerusalem under Jewish control (Luke 21:24)

Judgment signs:
- As it was in the days of Lot (Luke 17:28,30; Ezekiel 20:47; Zephaniah 1:18; Malachi 4:1; Revelation 8:7, 9:18)
- As it was in the days of Noah (Gluttony, drunknenness, illicit sex, corruption, violence) (Matthew 24:37; Genesis 6:11)
- Distress of nations (Luke 21:25)
- Hearts failing for fear (Luke 21:26)

Note: Most judgments described in the Book of Revelation, chapters 6-18, are identical to the signs found in Matthew 24 and Luke chapters 17 and 21.

SIN

Sin separates us from God (Isaiah 59:2). All sin results in judgment — the payoff is death and eventually, the Great White Throne Judgment (Romans 1:24-32; 6:23; 1 Corinthians 6:9,10; Galatians 6:7).

Revelation 21:8 and 22:15 provide a comprehensive picture of those who are damned for all eternity. They are:

The fearful — those who do not accept Christ to escape being ridiculed (Matthew 10:32)

Unbelievers — those who do not believe in and receive the Lord Jesus Christ (John 8:24)

The abominable — those who engage in wicked practices (Titus 1:16)

Murderers — those who kill others or hate (1 John 3:15)

Whoremongers — those who engage in fornication or consort with prostitutes (Ephesians 5:5-8)

Sorcerers — those who practice witchcraft, demonism, and follow after the occult. Sorcery comes from the Greek word *pharmakeia*, meaning "enchantment with drugs." Thus, drug users and even pushers are included in the guilty verdict for judgment.

Idolaters — those who worship or reverence anyone or anything other than the living and true God.

Liars — (John 8:44)

Dogs — false professors (2 Peter 2:21,22)

Homosexuals — (Romans 1:18-32)

The unrighteous — those who trust in self, works, a false religious system, or mere "religion" for salvation (Titus 3:5)

Fornicators — those who engage in premarital and extramarital sex (1 Corinthians 6:9,14-18)

The wicked — those who disregard all morality and moral standards.

The covetous — those who desire all things for themselves, especially that which belongs to others (Ephesians 5:5-8)

The malicious — those who willfully seek to destroy the person and property of others (James 1:26)

The envious — those resentful of others

Debaters — those who would rather argue with God than accept His truth

Deceivers — those who purposely mislead or betray others (2 Timothy 3:13)

Maligners — those who speak evil of, defame, or slander others (James 3:23)

Whisperers — those who gossip

Backbiters — those who constantly find fault with

others and speak maliciously about them

Haters of God

Despisers — those filled with contempt toward God and man

The proud — those possessing an excessively high opinion of themselves

Boasters — those who exalt self

Inventors of evil things

The disobedient to parents

Those without understanding (resulting from unconcern or rejection of the truth)

Covenant breakers — those who do not keep their word

Those whose affections are contrary to the laws of God and nature

The implacable — those exhibiting extreme stubbornness to the point of refusing to yield to the convicting power of the Holy Spirit (Proverbs 1:24-28; Acts 7:51,52)

The unmerciful — those who lack compassion (Ephesians 4:32)

Adulterers — those who practice extramarital sex (1 Corinthians 6:9,10)

The effeminate — generally younger persons in the process of becoming homosexuals or sodomites

Abusers of themselves with mankind — hardened homosexuals (Genesis 19:5)

Thieves — (1 Corinthians 1:10)

Drunkards — those given to and overcome by alcohol (Proverbs 20:1; 23:20,21; Luke 21:34; Romans 13:13; 1 Corinthians 6:10; Galatians 5:1,9-21; Ephesians 5:18)

Revilers — those who use abusive or contemptuous language

Extortioners — those who exact money from or take advantage of others through violence, threats, or misuse of authority

Persons who have practiced these sins then and who are still contaminated by the guilt of them, because they have not come to Christ, will be the ones judged before the Great White Throne.

Is there hope? *And such were some of you . . . but ye are*

justified in the name of the Lord Jesus, and by the Spirit of our God (1 Corinthians 6:11; 1 John 1:7; John 3:17).

There is not a sin that can keep a true believer out of heaven. God's Word clearly states that some Christians will be saved "so as by fire." They lose everything except their salvation. Because of it, they will be "ashamed" in Christ's presence (1 John 2:28). If believers were left behind at the Rapture because of some sin in their lives, who would the "ashamed" be at that investigative session? Rewards are lost because of disobedience and disobedience is sin (Romans 5:19; James 4:17).

666 (See Number of the Beast)

SOLOMON'S TEMPLE (See Temple)

SON OF MAN IN HEAVEN, SIGN OF (See Revelation)

SON OF PERDITION (See Antichrist . . . See Hell for Perdition)

SORCERY (See Signs)

SORROW

Christ's coming will undoubtedly be the most joyous event of the ages (Revelation 22:4), but it will be a time of intense and immense sorrow for some (1 John 2:28). At the Rapture, *all* believers are summoned into His presence for the Judgment Seat of Christ . . . the confident *and* the ashamed, those whose works are either good or bad (2 Corinthians 5:10,11). Those who "suffer loss" will shed many tears (see Rewards).

It is no small thing when true believers take their salvation for granted and their Saviour's commands lightly. Tears will flow because of neglected opportunities (Matthew 6:19,20), neglected holiness (1 Thessalonians 4:7; 2 Timothy 1:9; Hebrews 12:14; 1 Peter 1:16; Romans 13:14), and a meaningless life (see Rewards).

The result will be intermittent weeping for 1,007 years. It began at the Judgment Seat of Christ in heaven (which occurred at the beginning of the Tribulation Hour upon earth) and continues throughout the 1,000-year Millennium. After the Great White Throne Judgment of the world, God finally wipes all tears away from their eyes forever (Revelation 21:4).

Great sorrow and weeping is also sweeping the earth simultaneously during the Tribulation Hour. It is called the "beginning of sorrows" and the world and it's inhabitants will experience terrible times as never was (Matthew 24:21). The Jews also will "look on Him whom they have pierced and mourn" (Zechariah 12:10).

SPIRIT OF ANTICHRIST (See Antichrist, Spirit of)

SPOIL

When Russia invades Palestine, it will be for "spoil." This includes the mineral wealth of the Dead Sea as well as the wealth generated in Israel through industry and agriculture (Ezekiel 38:13).

STARS (See Signs)

SUN (See Signs)

SYMBOL

Something that represents another thing. In relation to prophecy, there are symbols used for persons, institutions, offices, events, actions, and things. The scriptural context usually makes it clear as to the intent of the symbol. When the common sense makes good sense, seek no other sense.

TARTARUS (See Hell)

TEARS (See Sorrow)

TELEVISION

Not until this generation with the invention of satellite television, did anyone know how it would be possible to beam an identical image to every nation on earth . . . even into private homes. Talk about a television spectacular! During the Tribulation Hour, the death of the two witnesses is observed by the entire world (Revelation 11:10) as their bodies are left lying in the street as Antichrist's forces celebrate around the world. Three and one-half days later, as the world continues to watch in horror, they stand up and vanish in a cloud (vss. 11,12). Next, an unprecedented earthquake hits the city and 7,000 celebrities (the interpretation of many scholars), big names among the elite, are killed (vs. 13). What a video extravaganza!

TEMPLE

The first place for Jewish worship ever built was Solomon's Temple (1 Chronicles 22,28,29; 2 Chronicles 2-7). This temple was destroyed by King Nebuchadnezzar of Babylon in approximately B.C. 590.

Seventy years later, it was rebuilt under Zerubbabel and Joshua. This second temple was desecrated by Antiochus Epiphanes, a Greco-Syrian ruler. He brought a pig into the Temple — an act which prefigured the final desecration to occur under Antichrist in the Tribulation temple and predicted to be "the Abomination of Desolation" (Matthew 24:15).

Herod the Great rebuilt and enlarged it in B.C. 20 or 21. The outer court was marked off from the inner one where only Israel was permitted to enter. No Gentile was allowed beyond that point.

In 70 A.D., Titus, the Roman general formed the Western nations of the old Roman Empire, went down to Jerusalem, smashed the Temple, and drove a million

T TEMPLE

Jews into every part of the earth.

Currently, during this Church Age, the body of each individual believer is the "temple" of the Holy Spirit (1 Corinthians 6:19,20) and God is to be glorified therein.

During the Tribulation period, a third temple will be erected in Jerusalem. It will be built during the Tribulation Hour. (This Temple will have nothing to do with the Church which is in heaven by now, Revelation 4:6). It's altar and attendants will be Jewish. Many Jews who do not turn to Christ during the Tribulation will return to Temple worship as in Old Testament times, including the sacrifice of animals. It may be that permission to erect this Temple in Jerusalem will be part of the peace agreement between the final world leader (Antichrist) and the Jews.

Although the peace contract with Israel is to last seven years (Daniel 9:27), halfway through, Antichrist will declare himself to be God and demand worship from the Jews in their own Temple (2 Thessalonians 2:4). The Image of the Beast will be set up in this Temple in a final act of blasphemy (Daniel 12:11) (see Abomination of Desolation). The Temple will fill with smoke, sealing off all entry for the rest of the Tribulation period.

The millennial Temple will be entirely different from the one used in the Tribulation. It will be used for the 1,000-year millennial period (Ezekiel 40-48), coming into existence shortly after Russia's invasion of Israel (Ezekiel 38,39) (see Temple, Ezekiel's).

There will be no temple in the New Jerusalem as God has chosen to dwell with man (Revelation 21:3,22).

TEMPLE, EZEKIEL'S

Temple worship will be reinstated along with its animal sacrifices during the Millennium. Just as the Lord's Supper symbolizes Calvary for Christians, animal sacrifices will symbolize Christ's sacrifice at Calvary for Israel.

The following are various theories and approaches to the understanding of Ezekiel's Temple (Ezekiel 40-48;

Isaiah 56:6-8; Jeremiah 33:15-18; Zechariah 14:16):
1. This temple is equated with Solomon's Temple
2. Ezekiel's Temple represents an ideal or pattern for the exiles as they rebuilt the restoration Temple
3. Messiah will build the Temple and inaugurate the Temple ceremonies
4. The Temple presents an allegorical view of Christ and the spiritual endowments of the Church in the Christian era
5. This Temple is a figure of all the redeemed of all ages who are worshipping God in heaven
6. This passage is a prophetic parable expressing principles of God's presence with His people
7. To the Dispensationalist, this is a literal temple with its sacrifices and priesthood during the Millennium

TEN NATION CONFEDERACY

This confederacy is pictured by the ten toes of Daniel's image (Daniel 2,7) and the ten horns of Revelation 13:1. Each of these nations was originally part of the old Roman Empire, and the leader will be Antichrist.

The final prophetical statement of Nebuchadnezzar's dream concerned the ten toes of iron and clay (see Nebuchadnezzar's Dream). The iron is still in existence at the endtime (Roman Empire), but in a deteriorated condition. (The ten toes have become mixed with clay ... a weakening.) The Roman Empire was never defeated, but fell through corruption. Since it still exists, it returns to power at the endtime in the form of a union of ten Western nations — and all ten nations will have been part of the original Roman Empire. Thus, the final power will be capitalism under ten Western nations in Europe. Once there are ten nations, the Bible teaches that a world dictator will arise out of the eleventh, twelfth, or thirteenth nation whose leader ousts three of the nations, reducing the alliance to the final ten nations signaling the return of the King (Daniel 2:44).

Then, in the days of this final alignment of the ten

original western nations, Christ comes to set up His kingdom (Daniel 2:44). From the hour that the leader of this ten nation confederacy signs a peace contract with Israel, one can count down on the calendar — seven years or 2,520 days — to the return of Christ as King. The final countdown is coming.

THEOCRATIC KINGDOM (See Kingdom)

THEOPHANY (See Angels)

THIRD HEAVEN (See Heaven)

THRONES

The Lord's throne is in heaven (Psalm 11:4). *Thy throne, O God, is forever and ever: the scepter of thy kingdom is a right scepter* (Psalm 45:6).

Envy of God's throne began with Satan: *For thou hast said in thine heart, I will ascend into heaven, I will exalt my throne above the stars of God . . . I will be like the most High* (Isaiah 14:12-14).

Revelation 4:1-6 describes God's throne room as still secure as one nears the end of time.

While on earth, Jesus taught His disciples to pray, *Thy kingdom come* (Matthew 6:10). That great event takes place in Revelation 19:16 when Jesus Christ ascends the throne of David (Isaiah 9:6,7; Luke 1:32) to begin His millennial reign. This throne belongs exclusively to the King of Kings and Lord of Lords. It is Christ's choice to share His throne (Revelation 4:20,21).

During the Millennium, the thrones are occupied by resurrected believers from Adam onward, inclusive of the last Tribulation martyr. Each has been a participant in the first resurrection. These saints are entitled to sit upon thrones because they are members of the royal priesthood (1 Peter 2:9; Revelation 20:4). Christ has made them kings and priests (Revelation 5:10).

The next throne we find is the Great White Throne when Jesus Christ judges all the resurrected wicked ones (Romans 2:16; John 5:27; Acts 17:31; 24:15; 1 Corinthians 15:22-24).

When last referred to, the throne of God is situated in the Holy City, the New Jerusalem, and a "pure river of water of life" proceeds out of it (Revelation 22:1).

THYATIRA (See Churches)

TIME, TIMES, AND HALF A TIME

The last three and one-half years of the Tribulation (Daniel 7:25; 12:7; Revelation 12:14). Time = one year. Times = two years. One-half time = 1/2 year. During the same period, we see other time designations: 42 months (Revelation 11:2; 13:5), 1,260 days (Revelation 11:3; 12:6) — all typifying three and one-half years.

TIMES AND SEASONS (See Chronology)

God controls the times and seasons (Daniel 2:21). It is not within man's knowledge (Acts 1:7) except as revealed by God's Word (1 Thessalonians 5:1,2) and the Holy Spirit (1 Corinthians 2:9-11) (see Prophetic Clock; Chronology).

TIMES OF REFRESHING

The Millennium, with its accompanying blessing and refreshing to Israel after the terrible Tribulation, following the return of Christ (Acts 3:19).

TIMES OF RESTITUTION

Same as the Times of Refreshing (Acts 3:21)

TIMES OF THE GENTILES

This is the period of Jewish captivity — beginning with the Babylonian captivity and ending with Armageddon at the conclusion of the Tribulation Hour. Events which have occurred since the Six Day War in

T TIMES OF THE GENTILES

1967 prove that Israel's present possession of Jerusalem is temporary. The hordes out of the North (Ezekiel 38,39), coming against Israel (Ezekiel 38:16), will attempt to capture Jerusalem. One can see the control of the city shifting back and forth before the final onslaught. Once Armageddon is finished, however, Jerusalem will be controlled by the Jews forevermore.

TRANSLATION

The removal of the believer from earth to heaven with a change in the body making the miracle possible (Hebrews 11:5; 1 Corinthians 15:50-52). "Translation" is often used in place of the word "rapture" (see Bodies, Glorified).

TREE OF LIFE

The tree of life bears 12 manner of fruits and produces them monthly. When Adam and Eve sinned by partaking of the tree of knowledge of good and evil (Genesis 2:17), God drove them out of the Garden of Eden to keep them from eating the fruit of the tree of life lest they would eat and live eternally in their sinful state.

The tree of life will appear again in the Holy City (Revelation 22:2). Undoubtedly this tree plays a part in promoting our endless existence, for even the leaves contain healing or health for the nations living under, or in the light of, the city. The word "health" is the proper translation, not healing. Since there is no sorrow, sickness, or pain, healing is unnecessary (see Holy City).

TRIBULATION

The Tribulation lasts seven years and is undoubtedly the worst bombardment of tragedy the earth will ever experience. God has a three-fold purpose for this period:

1. To save and allow many Jews who will enter the Millennium to experience the fulfillment of the kingdom promises to Israel made by God in the covenants

2. To save a multitude of Gentiles who will then popu-

late the millennial kingdom

3. To pour out judgment on unbelieving mankind and nations. The final 42 months or three-and-one-half year period is so terrifying that it is called the Great Tribulation (Revelation 7:14).

There is a reason the first half is more peaceful. Because Jesus Christ, the Prince of Peace, is soon to return, Satan, the great counterfeiter and super deceiver called Antichrist will present himself as the Messiah and be accepted! Satan will enter the body of a man and proclaim himself as God (2 Thessalonians 2:4). This Antichrist will come into prominence and power by presenting a "peace program" to the nations. The contracts are signed and confirmed (Daniel 9:27). However, in the middle of the seven-year period, the Antichrist dishonors his treaties and makes the last 42 months the bloodiest in world history. The Great Tribulation is a time of incomparable judgment from God (Daniel 12:1; Joel 2:2; Matthew 24:21). A total of 21 judgments fall upon the earth. They constitute three series of seven each and are described as the seal, trumpet, and vial (or bowl) judgments. This is the Time of Jacob's Trouble (Revelation 6,8,9,15,16) (see Judgments).

Revelation 8:7 and 9:18 clearly reveal a judgment of fire during the Tribulation. This coincides with Psalm 97:3; Isaiah 66:15; Ezekiel 20:47; Zephaniah 1:18; Malachi 4:1, and numerous other passages of Scripture. Both Old and New Testaments are in agreement concerning what seems to be a fiery, nuclear holocaust (Zechariah 14:12; Revelation 8:7; 9:18) (see Day of the Lord; Daniel's Seventieth Week).

I remain firmly convinced that the Church will be evacuated before the Tribulation judgment begins (see Rapture, Views of).

TRIBULATION ... ORDER OF
POLITICAL EVENTS

1. Rise of Antichrist as leader of a confederacy of ten western nations (Revelation 13:1)

2. Antichrist signs a seven-year peace contract with Israel (Daniel 9:27)

3. After 42 months, Antichrist breaks the contract (Daniel 9:27)

4. Russia invades Israel from the North (Ezekiel 38:15,16) at a time when Israel is at rest or peace (Ezekiel 38:11). (So this will not happen before the peace contract is in effect.)

5. Antichrist attempts to destroy God's people, the Jews (Revelation 12)

6. He destroys the world church that helped bring him to power (Revelation 17:16,17)

7. He proclaims himself as God (2 Thessalonians 2:4-11)

8. He himself is defeated at Armageddon (Revelation 19) and cast into the Lake of Fire (vs. 20)

The Tribulation period will end with the Battle of Armageddon and the return of the Lord Jesus Christ to earth (Revelation 19:11-16).

TRIBULATION SAINTS (See Martyrs)

TRIBULATION, VIEWS OF (See Rapture, Views of)

TRINITY, SATANIC (See Satan)

TRUCE BREAKERS (See Signs)

TRUMP OF GOD

Along with the shout and the voice of the archangel, the trumpet will sound to summon the dead in Christ and the living believers to heaven (1 Thessalonians 4:16). Apparently only believers will hear this trumpet as the Rapture is a silent exodus.

Trumpets in Scripture were used as a summons to assemble people (Numbers 10:2) and to announce God's divine presence (Exodus 19:16).

TRUMPETS (See Judgments)

TUBAL (See Russia)

TWINKLING OF AN EYE

A blink is calculated to be 11/100ths of a second. A half-blink becomes the twinkling of an eye. Just as Christ cried out, *Lazarus, come forth* (John 11:43), and immediately Lazarus arose from the dead, so shall the call ring out, *Come up hither* (Revelation 4:1) and the Church will be gone in a glorious flash (1 Corinthians 15:52) (see Rapture).

TYPOLOGY

An Old Testament person, institution, event, thing, office, place, or action intended by God to prefigure or foreshadow something that would be revealed at a later time. For example, Moses lifting up the serpent is the type (Numbers 21:9), while Christ, lifted up on the cross is the antitype (John 3:14) (see Interpretation, Methods of).

UNTHANKFUL U

UNHOLY (See Signs)

UNITED STATES (See Babylon)

UNTHANKFUL (See Signs)

VIALS (See Judgments)

WHORE (See Babylon)

WITCHCRAFT (See Sorcery)

WITNESSES, 144,000 (See Remnant)

WITNESSES, TWO

Two powerful prophets will appear in Jerusalem during the Tribulation period, guaranteeing the truth of the kingdom message of the 144,000 servants of God, adding to the irritation of the Antichrist. The message of Christ's return will be preached throughout the world. All will be made aware of the timetable of the end, the eventual fall of Antichrist, and the coming kingdom of Christ.

These two witnesses will be miraculously protected for three and one-half years. Their power to bring plagues will draw the attention of the world (Revelation 11:6). They will likely repeat Old Testament prophecies concerning the kingdom of Christ (Daniel 2:44,45).

When they have concluded their work, they will be slain and television will beam the sight of their dead bodies lying in the streets of Jerusalem to the world. After three and one-half days of the earth's rejoicing (Revelation 11:10), they will be resurrected and ascend to heaven in a cloud while their enemies watch, paralyzed with fear.

In determining who the two witnesses mentioned in Revelation 11:3 are, most biblical scholars have narrowed the choice down to either Elijah, Moses, or Enoch.

Malachi 3:2,3 and 4:5,6 predict that Elijah will come as one of those witnesses. It is corroborated by the fact that Elijah did not die a physical death but was taken up into heaven by a whirlwind and chariot of fire (2 Kings 2:9-11).

Moses appeared with Elijah on the Mount of Transfiguration (Matthew 17:3) which was a picture of future events. Many of the plagues of the Time of Jacob's Trouble are similar to those brought by Moses in the deliverance of Israel from Egypt. The Bible also tells us that Moses' body was preserved by God (Deuteronomy 34:5,6; Jude 9).

Like Elijah, Enoch did not die (Hebrews 11:5), and some think that his exemption from death was in view of his coming martyrdom during the Great Tribulation. His message must also be considered. Evidently this prophet had been given a revelation of the Second Coming of Christ and had announced it to his generation (Jude 14,15).

WOMAN OF REVELATION 12

Clearly the woman clothed with the sun and wearing a crown of 12 stars upon her head is Israel. The birth of this woman's (Israel's) son is predicted in Isaiah 66:7,8. Here we have the mother, Israel, bringing forth a man child who is none other than the blessed Lord Jesus Christ.

The same devil who attempted to destroy the woman's son in centuries past (Genesis 3:15) is now about to strike out against the woman herself via the greatest anti-Semitic purge in history. This is an age-long conflict. *And she brought forth a man child* [1,900 years ago] *who was to rule all nations with a rod of iron* [future]: *and her child was caught up unto God, and to his throne. And the woman fled into the wilderness, where she hath a place prepared of God, that they should feed her there a thousand two hundred and threescore days.*

During this final 42-month period, described as the Great Tribulation (Revelation 7:14), because of its intensity and immensity, the Children of Israel are protected by their God. He took care of them for 40 years as they wandered through the wilderness, and now He again proves His love to His ancient people by delivering them. They shall be saved out of it. By preservation — not by the Rapture as the Church experienced (Jeremiah 30:7; Daniel 12:1; Matthew 24:22).

WORLD CHURCH (See Babylon)

WORLD GOVERNMENT

Chapters 8 and 11 of Daniel state that knowledge and scientific advancement will be used by an international despot to control the nations of the world. Revelation 13:8,15-18 picture a world leader presiding over a world government whose international number is 666. He will take control of a newly built Jewish Temple in the Holy Land, proclaiming himself as the awaited Messiah (2 Thessalonians 2:4). The world will accept his proclamations out of fear as world war looks imminent. This leader (see Antichrist) will convince humanity that he has the answers to the world's ills and that he alone can bring peace. On the basis of peace negotiations between Israel and many nations (Daniel 9:27), he is accepted (see Ten Nation Confederacy).

There will be a new world monetary system and every person on earth will be given a number (Revelation 13:16-18). It looks as though this one-world despot will manipulate humanity with international computers. This sophisticated computer system will be fashioned in his likeness (see Image of the Beast). There will be no basic loyalty toward any country because whoever controls the monetary system will control the world's billions.

WORLD RULER (See Antichrist; World Government)

WORMWOOD

Revelation 8:11 tells us that a star, or meteor, named Wormwood, will strike the earth and one-third of our planet's water supply will become poisoned. God created every star, knows their locations and has named them (Job 9:9). He knows where the star, Wormwood, meaning "bitterness," is as well and will use it (Jeremiah 9:15).

ZION

There is a threefold meaning:

1. Jerusalem, the city of David
2. Millennial city of Jerusalem, capital city of Israel during the Millennium (Isaiah 2:3)
3. Heavenly city, New Jerusalem (Hebrews 12:22) (see Heaven; Jerusalem, New)

Bibliography

Pentecost, J. Dwight, *Things to Come* (Zondervan Publishing House, Grand Rapids, Michigan, 1964), Copyright 1958, Dunham Publishing Company.

Rouse, Donald R., *The Bible Student's Dictionary of Prophetic Terms* (Alpena, Michigan, 1986), Copyright Rev. Donald R. Rouse.

Van Impe, Jack, *Can America Survive?* (Royal Oak, Michigan, 1986), Copyright Jack Van Impe Ministries.

Van Impe, Jack, *11:59 . . . and Counting!* (Royal Oak, Michigan, 1983), Copyright Jack Van Impe Ministries.

Van Impe, Jack, *Heaven and Hell* (Royal Oak, Michigan), Copyright Jack Van Impe Ministries.

Van Impe, Jack, with Roger Campbell, *Israel's Final Holocaust* (Royal Oak, Michigan, 1979), Copyright Jack Van Impe Ministries.

Van Impe, Jack, *Prophecy* (Royal Oak, Michigan, 1982), Copyright Jack Van Impe Ministries.

Van Impe, Jack, *Revelation Revealed* (Royal Oak, Michigan, 1982), Copyright Jack Van Impe Ministries.

Van Impe, Jack, *Signs of the Times* (Royal Oak, Michigan, 1970), Copyright Jack Van Impe Ministries.

Van Impe, Jack, *The 80's, The Antichrist and Your Startling Future* (Royal Oak, Michigan, 1982), Copyright Jack Van Impe Ministries.

Note: New address
       Jack Van Impe Ministries
       P.O. Box 7004
       Troy, Michigan 48007